BEYOND HER
YES

BEYOND HER
YES

Reimagining Pro-Life Ministry to **Empower Women** and **Support Families** in Overcoming Poverty

Marisol Maldonado Rodriguez

BakerBooks
a division of Baker Publishing Group
Grand Rapids, Michigan

Published by Baker Books
a division of Baker Publishing Group
Grand Rapids, Michigan
www.bakerbooks.com

Printed in the United States of America

Library of Congress Cataloging-in-Publication Data
Names: Rodriguez, Marisol Maldonado, 1963– author.
Title: Beyond her yes : reimagining pro-life ministry to empower women and
    support families in overcoming poverty / Marisol Maldonado Rodriguez.
Description: Grand Rapids, Michigan : Baker Books, a division of Baker Publishing
    Group, [2023] | Includes bibliographical references.
Identifiers: LCCN 2022059181 | ISBN 9781540903556 (paperback) | ISBN
    9781540903648 (casebound) | ISBN 9781493443345 (ebook)
Subjects: LCSH: Church work with single parents—New Jersey. | Single mothers—
    Care—New Jersey. | RENEW Life Center. | Pro-life movement. | Church work
    with the poor. | Abortion—Religious aspects—Christianity.
Classification: LCC BV4438.7 .R63 2023 | DDC 259/.1—dc23/eng/20230208
LC record available at https://lccn.loc.gov/2022059181

23 24 25 26 27 28 29   7 6 5 4 3 2 1

In memory of my mom, Felicita,
whose face I see in every woman I serve.

Contents

Foreword

L ife after yes. Since saying yes to the role of director for a small pregnancy resource center in northern New Jersey fifteen years ago, I have seen the amazing potential of the Church—with a capital C—to extend hope and practical help to under-resourced, overwhelmed parents. Hope and help that save and change lives. Through the selfless generosity of countless individuals and churches, God has grown Lighthouse Pregnancy Resource Center to serve more and more women and couples facing unexpected pregnancies.

As we were being led to open the first pregnancy center for Paterson, our state's third-largest city and one of its most challenged urban areas, God led us to Marisol Rodriguez. This divine encounter included her three equally passionate colaborers in the founding of RENEW Life Center—Evelyn, Michele, and Sanyika. These women were familiar with the good work of pregnancy centers because they had served in them. But they also knew there was more good work that needed to be done after the precious "yes" was delivered into the arms of a courageous mom.

The services of a pregnancy center typically extend through pregnancy and a child's first year of life. But the complex issues and deep needs of under-resourced parents extend back several generations—and without extensive intervention, they will ripple forward to the next generations. Marisol and the cofounders of RENEW Life Center had experienced generational and situational poverty in their own lives. This gave them understanding, empathy, and a burning desire to equip other parents in poverty to thrive as they raise the next generation.

Lighthouse and RENEW joined forces to address the immense challenges mothers face as they struggle to say yes to a new life. We suspected we would be better together, and five years later, it seems we were right. We are *all* better together. God has made us so we need each other.

If your heart is already saying, *Yes, I want to do more for struggling parents and their children*, you will love this book's practical applications. If you have said yes to a life of following Christ but have never considered your responsibility to parents in poverty, I ask you to read this book with an open heart. And most of all, I pray God will use you—as He has used Marisol—to make a wonderful difference in this world.

Debbie Provencher
Executive Director, Lighthouse Pregnancy Resource Center

1

What If Our Pro-Life Perspective Is Too Narrow?

May your choices reflect your hopes, not your fears.

Nelson Mandela

As someone who had served in pro-life ministry for over a decade, I never thought that my view of pro-life ministry was too narrow. I was the client services director of a pregnancy resource center located in a large city in New Jersey. I had served as a volunteer there for almost ten years before I took on the director's role, and during that time, I thought I had developed a pretty good understanding of the pro-life cause and the many issues surrounding it. When I thought of pro-life ministry, I mainly thought of the abortion-minded women who came to the pregnancy center. My focus was to lead those women to choose life.

I was also concerned about sharing the gospel and with spreading the abstinence message to prevent teen pregnancies and to prevent repeat pregnancies for women who had already experienced an unplanned pregnancy. I was happy that we could supply them with diapers, wipes, and baby items, but what I did not know was that these women needed so much more than that initial material support.

On November 2, 2010, I received an email from one of our clients. She had been abortion minded when she visited us, but with counsel and encouragement from one of our volunteers, she made a choice for life. She had a college degree, she had a full-time career-path job, and she was a go-getter. So what I read in her email really rocked me to the core. Here is her message, shared with her permission:[1]

Subject: please advise me

Hello Marisol,

How have you been? I've been trying to stay close to God and do His will, but things seem not to be going as planned. I'm five months pregnant, and I'm scared. My debt-to-income ratio is so close that I'm living paycheck to paycheck, and I haven't found a way to budget getting any supplies for the baby to come. I'm not sure what I'm having (boy or girl), but I've been feeling depressed, and I've been crying a lot. I'm not sure where or who to turn to because my family has become too busy for me. I'm already stressing out due to my instability, and to add to the matter, my mom will not be able to babysit for me while I'm at work. I'm at my wit's end trying to plan and be able to survive on my check while providing for this baby that God put here for some reason.

I'm very sad because when I first spoke to Janet I was walking a thin line with the decision of having this baby, and now that I've made this decision, I'm not sure what to do to continue moving forward. Is there any way you can help me? Do you know where I can get the baby supplies, breast pump stuff, furniture, babysitting services, anything (quality materials and services for a low price)? I would like the baby to have something even if I have nothing. I have a TV that sits on top of a milk crate. I'm sleeping on a bed that hurts my back, and it's mismatched; one part is full, the other a queen, the base doesn't fit. I'm grateful I'm not sleeping on the floor. I don't want to be a failure, but I'm lost. Can you help me get back on track?

Amanda

I was stunned. I could not wrap my head around what I'd just read. I could sense her pain through her words. Initially, I was angry at myself—how did I drop the ball like that? I thought that because she had an education and a career, she would be okay. Pregnancy outside of marriage would put her in some difficulty; that was to be expected. But what I didn't think about was the fear and loneliness she was feeling. Worst of all, at five months pregnant, she was beginning to regret choosing to have her baby because she felt alone in that decision.

The email broke my heart, and Amanda's fear was well-founded, as there was a 40% chance that she would end up in poverty. What she earned as an elementary school teacher was fine for a single person, but for a family of two, it was far below what she needed to survive. That got me thinking: If this woman, who was much farther ahead educationally and economically than most of my clients, was struggling so badly, what was happening to my typical client? The thought scared me. The women I had seen week after week, month after month, for more than a decade felt like they were still sinking, and I hadn't realized it.

Although pregnancy resource centers provide expecting moms with many of the material items needed to care for a newborn baby, not all centers are able to provide them in the same capacity. The pregnancy center I worked at did not have the material resources that Amanda needed at that time. Her email was the impetus for me to take a closer look at what happens in the lives of women in poverty who choose life for their babies.

I believe pro-life Christians are right to make a focused effort to reach abortion-vulnerable women and save pre-born babies' lives. To that end, concerned Christians have relied heavily on pregnancy resource centers, which have some great success stories resulting from their diligent efforts. But our lifesaving efforts should not end with the saved life of the baby. We need to look at the big picture of the woman's life and her baby's future and seek to understand her context, the circumstances that make her abortion-vulnerable, and what she needs after she says yes to her baby's life. We have to consider the root of the problem—poverty itself—and how to alleviate it.

As I examined the traditional pro-life approach more closely, I realized that we had been shortsighted, and some of our foundational assumptions were rooted in four misconceptions:

1. *After a woman chooses life, she's going to be okay.*
   If I put myself in the shoes of a mother with a pregnant teenager or young adult daughter, I know I would do whatever it took to protect my grandchild's life and my daughter's future. But not every young woman facing an unplanned pregnancy has that type of support. A woman in poverty with a pregnant daughter could protect the life of her grandchild by encouraging her daughter to choose life, but she may not be able to help protect her daughter's future. Very often, the grandmother does not have the education or resources to do that.

   According to the website Single Mother Guide, "Among children living with mother only, 38.1% lived in poverty."[2] Additional research from the *National Vital Statistics Report* shows that the educational level of parents, particularly unwed mothers, is a key indicator of a child's likely educational level as well as other socioeconomic outcomes that will negatively affect them over the course of their lives.[3] Not only do these children have the disadvantage of being born to parents who have low levels of education, but because they are unmarried, the familial support structure is also greatly compromised.

2. *A pregnancy resource center is an all-encompassing solution.* It's not, and it's not meant to be. Pregnancy centers are more like medical triage units than long-term support. They are lifesavers, and they do a great job. Many of them have extended their services to include parenting classes and material support in the form of diapers, wipes, formula, and other basic baby items, but typically their services end a year after the baby is born. What happens after that? How does a young mom with a limited education learn to parent a difficult teenager? What about all the financial, emotional, and spiritual support she'll need along the way?

3. *A woman and her baby can survive on government assistance.* Besides the fact that this is not true, is that all we as Christians want? Do we want the woman and her baby to merely survive? To barely get by? I don't think that's what God has commissioned us to do. He has called us to abundant living, and we're called to share that abundant life with others.

   Gone are the days of blanket "welfare" in which all of an individual's basic survival needs were taken care of for the duration of their child's life. However, there are partial forms of government assistance, such as the Supplemental Nutrition Assistance Program (SNAP), formerly known as food stamps; Temporary Assistance for Needy Families (TANF), formally known as welfare; and Temporary Rental Assistance (TRA). They are not

all-encompassing programs but create some sense
of stability.

As of March 2022, "a majority (62%) of SNAP
households with children were single-mother
households," but "only 11% received cash benefits
from TANF."[4] Essentially this means that close to
90% of individuals who need additional financial
support do not receive it. Housing support has
limitations of up to two years—if it's available at
all. With rising food costs and lack of access to
full-service grocery stores in poverty-riddled areas
(often known as food deserts), there is much less
support and opportunity for a viable lifestyle. I
don't mean to suggest that financial security or
high levels of wealth are the answer, but a dignified
quality of life and a spirit of hope are not unrea-
sonable minimums to be met.

4. *Only unmarried and non-Christian women are
abortion-vulnerable.* I have seen many couples at
the center who are married or engaged and are
considering abortion. Why? Because they're just
not ready for a child right now, they want to buy
a house first, or they want to pay off their student
loans or get their careers off the ground.

I also know firsthand that a woman can regularly attend church and still be considering an
abortion. I believe one of the main reasons many
women consider abortion is they fear losing
something else that is very important. A woman
in church has the same fears as others (losing

financial stability, her education, a relationship, etc.), plus the added fear of judgment and being ostracized from her church family if she reveals her pregnancy. If she's a young woman and her parents hold a position in the church, then she fears the shame the pregnancy will bring on her family and the impact it will have on her parents serving in the church.

Despite the evidence to the contrary, it's easy to hold these misconceptions, especially if one hasn't experienced poverty. RENEW cofounder Sanyika Calloway explains:

> Those who have never lived in poverty don't know the hurdles, the boundaries, and the detours that having an unplanned pregnancy place on a woman in poverty. So it's easy to assume or think that once she chooses life, she's going to be okay, but she's not going to be okay because she comes from a background of poverty. She has a limited education, limited options, limited life experiences, and greatly diminished chances for change, progress, or success.[5]

If a woman comes from a middle-income background and becomes pregnant as a teenager or college student, she will most likely have the support she needs to finish her college education. Her parents will rearrange their schedules, hire babysitters, and provide financial support. They will do whatever it takes to ensure she has a stable future. But if a woman doesn't have that support system as a pregnant teenager or young adult, then high school stops and college never begins. Instead, she enters a cycle of hopelessness and despair where one poor choice warrants another, and she doesn't know the way out. Moving beyond that reality becomes the exception rather than the rule.

Living in poverty does not merely mean struggling to provide basic needs due to a lack of financial stability. It is an all-encompassing condition that affects how a person feels, how they think, how they form relationships, how they function as parents, how they practice self-esteem, how they view their own future and the future of their families, and how others view them.

Addressing poverty is important because women in poverty are targeted for abortion. We have to understand what poverty is like for individuals and for families if we want to better understand what they truly need to not only choose life but also lead an abundant life. When we are looking at them through the lens of our middle-class lives, we assume that they have the opportunity to make the same choices we do but choose something different. This is not the case. When we understand the reality of poverty, we will have a greater impact on saving lives. We will be able to see the whole picture of the woman's life, not just her unplanned pregnancy and the next few choices in front of her. We'll have an idea of what her history may be and the possible course of her future. Then we can better address and quell her fears of the life of poverty she may feel trapped in.

According to research compiled from national studies, in 2020,

> Almost one third (27.7%) of single mother families were "food insecure," about one-ninth (11.7%) used food pantries, one third spent more than half their income on housing, which is generally considered the threshold for "severe housing cost burden." Families headed by single mothers are among the poorest households, [and] more than a third lived in poverty, and as such, are extremely vulnerable to homelessness.[6]

If we care about the pro-life issue, we have to care about poverty. Period. They are inextricably linked. Can you see that if we separate the two, we're only doing half the job God has called us to? It's no wonder we will throw our hands up in disbelief when the same girl keeps coming back pregnant again and again.

The majority of unplanned pregnancies and abortions happen to women in poverty. If we want to stop or reduce unplanned pregnancies and abortions among this population, we must address poverty itself. Poverty is not a religious issue, although Philippians 2:4 tells us, "Let each of you look not only to his own interests, but also to the interests of others." It's not a political issue, though we should vote for leaders who support our biblical view. Fundamentally, poverty is an economic issue.

After that harsh but necessary wake-up call from Amanda's email, I began to look more closely at the lives of my clients. I noticed things I never had before, although they were obvious all along. Without even knowing it, I had gotten into a pattern of seeing only the problems I expected to see, rather than seeing each new individual as exactly that—someone I had never met before, with their own set of struggles, fears, doubts, and worries totally unique to them.

Perspective is a powerful thing, and once we see something with a new awareness, it's hard to unsee it. The vast majority of women who walked into my center lived in poverty. Although I had been raised in poverty in that same city, I had forgotten what it was like for my mother to raise eight children completely on her own. I felt the Lord telling me I had to remember the shame, fear, and frustration of being poor. In that remembering, the Lord broke my heart, then built me back up and gave me an expanded calling.

Generational and Situational Poverty

I've been speaking of poverty in general terms, but I would like to make some important distinctions. There are two types of poverty: generational and situational. Women experience generational poverty when they come from a background of poverty for two generations or more. Situational poverty is when an event such as the loss of a job, an illness, or a divorce throws a person into poverty. When a woman experiences situational poverty, it's easier to get out because she has the skills, contacts, and resources to get back on her feet with some effort and time. When a woman comes from generational poverty, she doesn't have any of that. She faces a huge knowledge gap because the life skills she needs to overcome poverty are not covered in school, not modeled by her family, and not seen in the lives of those she interacts with, and so they're not known.

Middle-income families naturally pass down to their children the skills needed to live productive and economically stable lives. In poverty, the skills that are passed down are based on survival. That's what a woman's parents know how to do well, and that's what is taught or, in most cases, caught through the experiences of her life. So while middle-income families often experience greater cycles of wealth creation, families in poverty often experience greater cycles of entrenched poverty. However, we can use the unplanned pregnancies women are facing to save lives, save souls, and interrupt poverty patterns for generations to come.

I love Isaiah 58, in particular verses 6–9:

> Is not this the kind of fasting I have chosen:
> to loose the chains of injustice
>   and untie the cords of the yoke,
> to set the oppressed free
>   and break every yoke?
> Is it not to share your food with the hungry
>   and to provide the poor wanderer with
>   shelter—
> when you see the naked, to clothe them,
>   and not to turn away from your own flesh and
>   blood?
> Then your light will break forth like the dawn,
>   and your healing will quickly appear;

then your righteousness will go before you,
    and the glory of the LORD will be your rear
      guard.
Then you will call, and the LORD will answer;
    you will cry for help, and he will say: Here am
      I. (NIV)

God gives us clear instructions on how we should address those facing poverty and oppression. He then tells us why we should do it—because our well-being is tied to theirs.

Bringing Options to Light

Often when I sit across from women considering an abortion, the stories I hear are the same. She had a dream. Maybe her goal was to be the first person in her family to graduate from high school or college. Perhaps it was to have a career and help her mom and siblings have better lives. She aspires to something that no one in her family has ever been able to do. She hasn't seen it role-modeled. She doesn't know how to get from here to there. But what she's sure of is that this pregnancy will put an end to her dream.

At that moment, we as the Church have the opportunity to tell this woman that there's a third option—an option where she can choose life and her dreams as well. But we have to show her that it is possible. If she's willing to do the hard work of bringing a child into the world, raising that child, and pursuing her goals, then there are people who will come alongside her in solidarity, providing consistent support and resources to help her make her dream a reality. When we show her that we are the guardians of her dreams and the shepherds of her soul, we show her that we love her, her baby, and their future. They all matter to God and to us.

The Difference One Church Can Make

I was born to a single woman in Puerto Rico who already had six children. Her life was hard. She was orphaned by the age of nine, she never went to school, and other than cooking, cleaning, and raising children, she didn't have any particular work skills. She was wholly dependent on the man in her life for survival.

My father, the latest man in her life, was an abusive, violent man, but she was thankful that he kept her and her children fed, housed, and safe from *other* predators. In 1965, my father brought us all to New Jersey. Here, in one generation, the course of life for my mother's descendants changed forever! Her children went from being another generation to experience abject poverty, no education, and no marriages to being educated and skilled professionals, spouses, and homeowners who never spent a day on welfare once they reached adulthood.

How did she do it? She didn't. At least not on her own. She stepped into a church, and that made all the difference in our world.

My mother was introduced to the Lord in Puerto Rico by a neighbor named Doña Mery. My older sisters told me that she was a very kind older woman with long white hair in a bun. Every time Doña Mery saw my mother outside hanging laundry on the clothesline, she would come out to tell her about Jesus and invite her to church. After many of these conversations, my mother accepted her invitation and went to church with her. That day was the beginning of a new life for us.

When my family arrived in New Jersey, the first thing my mother did was look for a church. She found a small storefront church in Newark. It was a poor church, it didn't have many resources, and there were only a couple of middle-income families who were part of the congregation. But the members were kind and made us feel welcome.

At that time, we lived in a tiny two-bedroom apartment. My mom converted the dining room into a third bedroom for herself and my father. The kids were crammed into the other two bedrooms. That was my life. We barely survived, but life was the same in every other house in our neighborhood, so I thought it was normal. What I knew wasn't normal was my father's violent and erratic behavior, but I never spoke about it. In fact, I don't remember us talking about it at home among ourselves either. That was just the way he was, and we accepted it. We kept our heads down and our mouths shut and stayed clear of him as best we could. That is, until our church got involved in my mother's life.

The more the congregation found out about what was happening in our home, the more they got involved. The women rallied around my mother with love and support. As the pastor made a plan to have my father removed from the home, others in the church taught my mother about social services and how to apply for them so that she didn't have to rely on my father for survival. Otherwise, she would have never agreed to have him taken from our home.

I was only a little girl, so that plan to have him removed wasn't discussed with me, but I remember the day it was put in motion. Our pastor sat nervously on our couch, waiting for my father to come home from work, while two police officers were stationed outside our home in case things became violent, which most certainly they would. I remember my mother was very scared; she was terrified of my father. But she put her trust first in God and then in her new family.

Although there was much fear and chaos, the plan worked. My father got the message that my mom was not alone anymore, and she was not fair game for his rage and abuse. There was now a group of people who surrounded her and supported her. The few times he attempted to make his way back into our home, he was reminded that things had changed. A new life had begun for us. And all it took was the body of Christ to see, listen, and take action boldly. From then on, my mother and her children were finally free of the tyranny of my father.

Although she probably did not feel that way at the moment, my mother was one of the lucky ones. Raising eight children as a single mother might not have sounded like a dream arrangement, but she was surrounded by people determined to love, protect, and nurture her and her family. They kept away the elements that threatened to disrupt her making progress. Her blessing was in finding the church before the situation got so bad that the way out was no longer clear.

Just as important as the church's role was my mother's desire to have a better life and her willingness to work for it, even when times were tough and things seemed impossible. She was willing to accept that the way out of poverty was not by finding a man to take care of her but rather by empowering herself to work out of the situation and empowering her children to never have to live the same life.

2

Saying Yes in Poverty

Wisdom consists of the anticipation of consequences.

Norman Cousins

hat happens when we don't recognize the relationship between overcoming poverty and pro-life ministry, and how does that affect our ministry? First, women and children needlessly suffer, and that suffering extends for generations with far-reaching social and spiritual implications for the world. And second, pro-abortion advocates can use our narrow view as evidence to support their assertion that we care only about the baby. Most pro-life ministries do care for both women and babies. When they spare a baby from abortion, they also spare a woman from a lifetime of regret and possible serious consequences to her physical and emotional well-being. However, an expanded view that understands the connection between poverty and unplanned pregnancies allows us to better serve women and give them the education and support they need to avoid the long-term suffering brought about by chronic instability.

Women in Poverty and Unplanned Pregnancies

When RENEW cofounder Sanyika Calloway and I first began exploring the relationship between unplanned pregnancies, poverty, and abortion, Sanyika came across a book titled *A Framework for Understanding Poverty* by Ruby K. Payne.[1] Dr. Payne is an expert on the mindsets of economic classes. Her book helped us better understand the history of poverty among the women we serve. In an interview, Dr. Payne discussed the relationship between unplanned pregnancies and poverty.

> **Me:** With free or reduced-cost contraceptives made available to people in poverty, why are there so many unplanned and unmarried pregnancies in poverty?
>
> **Dr. Payne:** To not have a pregnancy, you have to plan, and the more unstable your environment, the more difficult it is to plan—coupled with the fact that criminologists will tell you they can predict the amount of violence in the neighborhood by two things: the adults' educational attainment level and the number of households who do not have men living in them permanently. This leaves women in these neighborhoods with a need for protection. If

you want protection and you want a man in your household, what's going to be his incentive to stay with you? If you love that man and want to show him that you love him, you will give him a child because it's proof of his masculinity. That's not understood in the middle class at all.

Me: Can you expand on the reality of women in poverty needing protection?

Dr. Payne: People who have never experienced poverty do not understand that if you're a female in poverty and you live in a high-poverty area, you have to have protection or you are everybody's game. You're a target for everybody. And not only are you a target for everybody, but so are your children. You can't protect your children alone. They're vulnerable because, in poverty, the clear understanding is if there's no man around, you're fair game. The closer you get to survival, the more you're going to use physical approaches to survive.

When the media talks about single mothers in poverty, they talk about the fact that they don't have money. Sometimes they talk about the fact that they don't have time to be with their children because they're working two jobs, but it's an even deeper issue—they don't have anybody to protect them or their children. The reality is that the protective mechanism for women in poverty oftentimes is to go to a man for protection. A lot of times, the whole discussion is about money and time. But at the heart of the matter is the fact that if you want to survive a high-poverty neighborhood, protection is huge.[2]

As I listened to Dr. Payne talk about protection, so many conversations I have had with women at RENEW came into focus. I felt convicted remembering the times a woman had returned to the center pregnant and I rolled my eyes and thought, *Here she is again—another man, another baby.* The decisions my mother made regarding men also came into focus. She had five daughters. Her involvement with my father, a man who was well-known and feared in our area, ensured her daughters' safety. We were untouchable in our community, but it was at the expense of my mother's well-being—she endured abuse for our sake. My mother and the women returning to the center weren't weak-willed women; rather, they were striving to ensure their own survival and that of their children.

Creating space for a woman in poverty to articulate how she feels has brought about some of the most emotionally powerful conversations I've ever had. For many of the women who sit across the room from me, it is the first time someone asked them what effect choosing life has had on them. Once they begin talking, the trickle of words and phrases turns into a raging river of thoughts and feelings. One of the women we serve put it this way:

When girls like myself choose life and then find ourselves in difficult situations, we lean on the wrong support—another man, for example. Then we end up pregnant again by a man who is not providing for us. How do we come back to you and say, "Oh, you know what, Marisol, I did it again"? It's a cycle. We're looking for help, we're looking for a need to be met, so we gravitate to a man, and we cling to him.

What she shared is not lost on me, although it took a decade for me to better understand it. When we have a need, we will do whatever it takes to fill it. For many women in poverty, their father being absent compounds their fear of abandonment, so their determination to fill that void becomes desperate and overwhelming. They grasp at any chance for safety and security, even if it's only for a short while.

Families in Poverty

But what about the other part of this equation? What about the person whose only fault is being born into a situation where poverty is thrust upon them? They suffer in ways that they might not remember but that become ingrained in their identities. The *Psychiatric Times* reports on poverty's effect on the physical and mental health of both mother and baby:

> Individuals who experience poverty, particularly early in life or for an extended period, are at risk for a host of adverse health and developmental outcomes throughout their life. Poverty in childhood is associated with lower school achievement; worse cognitive, behavioral, and

attention-related outcomes; higher rates of delinquency, depressive and anxiety disorders; and higher rates of almost every psychiatric disorder in adulthood. Poverty in adulthood is linked to depressive disorders, anxiety disorders, psychological distress, and suicide.[3]

If you can imagine the feeling of being stuck in quicksand and struggling to get out, you can imagine what it feels like to live in poverty. Every slight movement to escape is met with the equal possibility of being sucked farther down if you fail. Now imagine a child in that same scenario, born into poverty without even realizing the danger they face from day one, never grasping that their normal isn't what life should look like.

The *Psychiatric Times* also explains the role of neighborhood deprivation on the lives of these families:

Findings indicate that geographically concentrated poverty—often in urban areas—is particularly toxic to psychiatric well-being. Signs of social and physical disorder often characterize poor neighborhoods, which can cause stress, undermine health-promoting social ties, and affect the mental health of people who live there. Neighborhood deprivation has been associated with many of the same mental health outcomes as poverty, even while controlling for individual poverty.

Additionally, a 2017 report from the Urban Institute states that only 62% of children in poverty get a high school diploma by the age of 20.[4] These children often start life at a disadvantage that makes achievements later in life more difficult.

I once counseled an eighteen-year-old woman to choose life. Fifteen years later, she came back with her pregnant daughter, hoping that she would also choose life. I'm glad the mother remembered us and came back, but her visit confirmed that her family's circumstances hadn't been fully transformed. Her life was not changed to the point where she could teach or model to her children how to follow a different path. As a result, the new generation received the same modeling and message from the older generation.

Single Moms in Poverty

Single motherhood is hard and often leads to poverty and limited opportunities, and these effects are even more intense for teen moms. According to a study from the National Conference of State Legislatures (NCSL), teen pregnancy is strongly linked to poverty. Some "63 percent of teen mothers receive public assistance within the first year of a child's birth. Fifty-two percent of mothers on welfare had their first child in their teens."[5] Additionally, "teen mothers are less likely to complete high school or college, and are therefore less likely to find well-paying jobs," and so "the economic consequences of dropping out of school often contribute to the perpetual cycle of economic hardship and poverty that can span generations."[6] To make matters worse, child support, which generally represents a vital income source for single mothers, is usually not in play because young fathers often have limited educational attainment and earning potential as well.

RENEW cofounder Sanyika Calloway reflects on feeling financially and emotionally trapped due to her unplanned pregnancy at the age of sixteen:

> Depending on your perspective, you can think this is awesome. I am carrying a life. I am bringing a new life into this world. But for me, it was a life sentence that quite literally felt like an albatross. It was a weight that I did not want to carry. I could not see a future. I could not see completing high school. I could not see leaving the small town that I grew up in. I could not see college. I could not see a life that was full and felt fulfilled as a single mother. So, I chose to have an abortion. For me, it seemed like the only way out of the prison I already felt trapped in.[7]

Often the Church and pro-life supporters don't realize the lack of opportunities a single mom experiences. We think that she knows how to get a job, that she can find childcare, or that she can go back to school. But we're talking about families who don't even have internet access or a computer in the house! She can't do distance learning; she can't do college online. When we don't understand this absence of opportunities and resources, we say things like, "Why doesn't she just leave him?" But if she leaves him, who will protect her and her children in their dangerous neighborhood? In our middle-class lives, we don't have to think about that.

Or we might ask, "Why doesn't she just get a job?" Well, when her mother never had a job and her grandmother never had a job, she doesn't know what getting a job looks like. How does she write a résumé? How does she fill out a job application? How does she handle a job interview and the stress that comes from being in an environment and situation she was never taught to navigate?

I remember walking home from school as a teenager and looking around at my neighborhood. It was unattractive and bleak, and I thought, *Is this what I want for my life? Is this all there is for me?* Because I had friends that lived in middle-class families, I saw that people could do better, and I decided I wanted better. Although I never faced a teen pregnancy, I didn't know how to get from where I was to where I wanted to be. No one in my family had done it before.

Fortunately, there were people in my church who had a vested interest in my future. Shortly after I graduated from high school, one of the men at the church asked me, "Marisol, what are you going to do with your life?" Honestly, I didn't know I had a choice. When you come from generational poverty, life just happens to you. There's no planning, no dreaming; you just live and roll with the punches. So I answered him, "Well, I'm working at Rite Aid, but other than that, I don't know." The thought that there was a life beyond that was foreign to me.

If a child is growing up without a father, and their mother has no social support, no community, and no healthy male presence to fill the father's role, then we shouldn't be surprised when the child doesn't know how to improve their condition or becomes involved in unhealthy behaviors that create a sense of belonging and safety at the expense of their personal freedom and dignity. Crime, poverty, violence, abuse, and unstable and unhealthy family relationships are only some of the experiences that can lead young people to join gangs or turn to prostitution, stripping, and other morally corrupt, short-term solutions for income.

Absent fathers and unsafe communities create a big, empty hole that needs to be filled, and that hole should be filled by the Church. If we don't take the initiative, gang members and "street influencers" will step in to meet the family's need for community and safety and so perpetuate the problem.

Adolescents Living in Fatherless Homes[8]

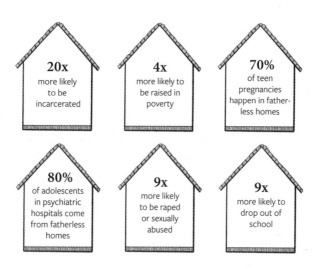

20x more likely to be incarcerated

4x more likely to be raised in poverty

70% of teen pregnancies happen in fatherless homes

80% of adolescents in psychiatric hospitals come from fatherless homes

9x more likely to be raped or sexually abused

9x more likely to drop out of school

We must recognize that poverty is not just an economic disadvantage; it's a life of vulnerability and hopelessness. The feelings of vulnerability and despair can lead single moms to form unhealthy relationships with men to gain a sense of safety. Unfortunately, these relationships don't last very long and often leave her with another unplanned pregnancy.

Single mothers are at high risk for poor mental and physical health, along with a sense of despair and helplessness, all of which are passed to their children. Youth living in impoverished neighborhoods are at risk of becoming hopeless about their future and engaging in violent or unhealthy behavior. When a young person has no future to look forward to, and when their role models are the gang members and drug dealers on the street, how can they be expected to live differently without having different role models, different tools, and a different reality to aspire to?

Recognizing these obstacles doesn't mean it's easy to address them. Not everyone that we meet at the pregnancy center who says yes to life is going to want the mentoring support and discipleship that we're offering them. But some will, and those are the ones we have to focus on. We have to invest time and resources in the moms and dads who are craving community, who are craving relationships, and who are desperate for someone to demonstrate that they will walk alongside them for the long haul.

Our message must be, "I am not a temporary person in your life. I am here for however long you allow." We're asking them to make a long-term commitment by choosing life, and I'm asking the Church to make a long-term commitment as well. To break the poverty-perpetuated cycle of poor education and physical and mental health issues that women navigating unplanned pregnancies face, we need to take a comprehensive approach to improving their quality of life. Through social services referrals, meaningful relationships, and committed discipleship, I believe we can work with families to help them build a sustainable future.

In chapter 1, I mentioned that pregnancy resource centers are like medical triage units. Their job is to stop the bleeding and get the client resuscitated. As a result, improving the mother's and child's quality of life must become the job of the Church. Without the hands-on support of committed and caring believers— something my mother and I received—women in poverty aren't able to carve a new path for their families.

3

Am I My Sister's Keeper?

Caregiving often calls us to lean into love we didn't know possible.

Tia Walker

Whether a child is in the womb and months from being born, or six months old and adorable, or a sixteen-year-old young woman who comes into our center feeling scared and alone—YES, we are her keeper. How are we actively showing our care and commitment to her keeping? Where can we show up to demonstrate that commitment? What is our responsibility as Christ-followers, not only on the front lines of the pro-life issue but also in our communities? How can we as pro-life people seek justice for women of all ages and life situations? I want us to consider both spiritual and practical answers to these questions—answers that I believe should inform the Church's pro-life work.

No God—No Hope

Many women trapped in generational poverty feel hopeless. They don't have the education, resources, or support to change their circumstances, and as a result, unplanned pregnancies continue to be a part of their lives and their children's lives.

Those of us who know Christ know that hopelessness comes primarily from not knowing God and knowing He gives us true hope in all situations. Imagine not having that hope in Christ and living in an economically depressed area where everything is bleak and dark. Hope cannot be produced out of thin air; something must initiate it. I believe that to initiate hope, we must introduce individuals to Christ. But we can't stop there. We must also bolster that introduction with support that they can see, hear, and touch. Church must move from something we do once a week to a lifestyle we live out every day of the week. Darkness and despair are ever present for those who don't know God, so we must surround these families as believers who are the hands and feet of Jesus in a world that is hurting and crying out for help.

When we bring hope to a mom, we bring hope to her children, because she will pass it down to them. I once heard this wonderful quote: "Your ceiling becomes your children's floor." As someone who comes from poverty, I get that. I started out educationally, economically, and spiritually at the highest level my mom had attained. Unfortunately for me, that was pretty low, but it would have been a lot worse without the support of our local church.

The early involvement of the church in my family's life made it possible for me to raise my ceiling so that my children would never experience poverty or its devastating effects the way I had.

I am passionate about helping moms believe that they can raise their ceilings so that their children—the ones we encouraged them to bring into the world—are not starting where they did. Instead, those children are starting from a different place, an elevated place, a place where the light can shine through.

Leading people to hope is hard; helping them keep hope alive is even harder. Hope evaporates the moment a mom hears gunshots outside her window or smells marijuana in the hallway. It takes an ongoing relationship to lead a mom to the source of hope and to keep reminding her that her hope is in Christ, not her environment.

Giving Hope and Saving Lives

Anna, a sidewalk advocate, spends a couple of days a week standing outside an abortion clinic, hoping to talk to the women who are about to enter it. It's a tough job. In my opinion, it's the toughest job in pro-life ministry. She's out there day after day, most times alone. But she's driven by the passion of giving a woman one last chance to reconsider her decision.

It's a great day when a woman stops and listens to Anna's message of life. That also gives Anna the opportunity to hear the woman's story and what led her to the clinic in the first place. She says it's almost always the same story:

"I don't have a job." "I'm about to get evicted." "I can barely survive myself. How am I going to afford a baby?" The list of needs goes on and on, which makes sense because one of the main reasons women give for considering an abortion is financial instability.[1] Anna explains: "I can't say, 'Hey, I know it's tough, but you should have the baby anyway. Abortion is a sin.' I have to offer her real, tangible help. I have to say, 'We care about you and the baby; there is help available for you to get on your feet; you are not in this alone.' That's what gets a woman to turn away from the abortion clinic."

Tom is a young man who recently started joining Anna on the sidewalk of the abortion clinic. He talks to the men who are accompanying the women to the clinic. Early on, he got his first save! Tom was super excited that God used him in this way. He spoke to a man named Alex, who was walking into the clinic with his girlfriend, Priscilla. He told Alex about the developmental stage of the baby, which meant there was a beating heart.

Alex said that his hours had been cut at work, and he was trying to find more work but hadn't had any luck. Priscilla was also out of work because of the at-risk pregnancy and her need to be off her feet. The basement apartment they had been living in turned out to be an illegal rental. The owner of the house had been fined, and now they had to move out within sixty days. They had nowhere to go and no money.

Tom said what he thought he should: "We care about you and the baby. There is help available for you to get on your feet, and we can help you find a place to live. You are not in this alone." He offered to take them to the local pregnancy center, and in that instant, Alex told Priscilla, "Let's go with him."

What stood out to me when I heard this story was how quickly this couple trusted a total stranger's offer to help, which leads me to believe that they really didn't want an abortion. They grasped the first and only offer for help they'd received. They just couldn't see how they would get out of the mess on their own.

These problems grow out of the brokenness of our culture. We have to answer Alex's and Priscilla's real needs with tangible assistance.

It was exciting that Tom made his first abortion clinic save, but he was about to face a problem that he didn't see coming. When he promised that "we" would help Alex and Priscilla get on their feet and find a place to live, who exactly did he mean? Was he referring to government social services? If so, then the couple might be on a waiting list for years. Was he referring to the pregnancy center? Pregnancy resource centers provide a wide range of support and services and may refer people to resources or shelters. But generally speaking, they are not in the housing business, and that's okay because that's not their primary mission.

When Tom spoke to Anna about Alex's and Priscilla's needs, he quickly found out that "we" was a huge vacuum. When Tom made the bold proclamation of additional support, he was confident that he was just the first runner of a lifesaving relay team. He assumed that every leg of the journey had someone with open arms and resources who would do everything possible to help Alex and Priscilla.

He would pass the baton to the next runner—the pregnancy center—and the needs of this couple and countless others like them would be met. All he had to do was go back to the abortion clinic and try to rescue the next baby; his job was done. The pregnancy center would do its work, and then it should be able to pass the baton to the Church. The Church would be the final runner of this race, where the finish line is crossed and lives are not just saved but transformed through Jesus Christ.

But seldom is the journey that easy, even with so many people fully committed to the cause.

Relay Race for Life

In an interview, Pastor Tim Chicola, senior pastor of The Crossing Church in Livingston, New Jersey, explained how the Church ought to run this race.

> **Me:** What do you see as the role of the Church in helping women and men choose life?
>
> **Pastor Tim:** It is incumbent upon the Church to teach that we have to preserve life, and especially when we're talking about life in the womb. If we don't protect it, then we are really part of the problem. . . . If we say that we desire to see Christ formed in people, then we have to be supportive of life and supportive of women who choose life. I think it's a foundational issue.
>
> **Me:** You said that the Church should support the women who choose life, but how?

Pastor Tim: I think there has to be education. Depending on a woman's upbringing, she may not have received the education she needs to create a healthy and stable home life for herself and her baby. And she also needs biblical teaching.

Beyond education, we have to get our hands dirty, as Jesus did. Sure, He sent the twelve apostles out two by two, but when they went out to do ministry, it was a ministry that He was already doing. When He sent them out, it was not to do something they had never seen before. We need to get in there, so to speak, and one by one rescue these women educationally, spiritually, emotionally, and physically. After the birth, that's when the work really has to begin, and unfortunately, a lot of times the Church doesn't know how or where to help.

When I was younger, I remember going to abortion clinics and standing in front, telling women, "Don't get an abortion." If you were ever successful, you'd go "Hallelujah," high-five, and then that was it. I went home, and that was the end of everything. But it was just the beginning for this woman and child.

The challenge that these women face many times, especially if they've been in a crisis pregnancy situation, is that they don't have strong support at home; they don't have emotional support, spiritual support, or financial support. Lots of times, when they decide to do what is right—to preserve the image of God—their troubles just begin.

[In] the good Samaritan story, the Samaritan saw a man who was beaten up and was in need, so he helped. If those who are sensitive to the Spirit of God know that there is a need and have the where-withal to help, if we don't help, then for me, it is a sin.

Now, that does not mean we can cure all the world's ills, but we are called as Christians not only to preach the gospel and set the captives free, set hearts free, unshackle them, but to also work for the betterment of culture, society, and injustice. We are called to participate in those things that make life better here on earth. The gospel calls me to love the Lord God with all my heart and all my strength and to love my neighbors as myself. So even if someone is not a Christ-follower, I am called to help him or her as I am able. I think the Church has long been weak in the post-decision-making process that a woman enters often alone. God forbid that we continue to do that anymore. I think we've seen enough; we know enough, and I think it's time to participate in the critical areas of feeding, housing, clothing, and finding jobs.

Me: You mentioned that you felt the Church has been weak in the area of support after the "yes." Can you tell me how the Church can improve on that?

Pastor Tim: I don't think we have a choice but to expand our involvement in the areas I mentioned: feeding, housing, clothing, and finding jobs; often, churches don't know how to go about doing that. . . . [But we want] to be able to see someone make a fair wage, to be able to raise their children well, to be able to pay for their housing. . . . When people move out of poverty, society is better, and their children's outcomes will be better. One of the loudest criticisms the pro-life movement receives from pro-abortion advocates is that we only care about the baby. Our response has to be a tangible one that wraps its arms around the entire situation and offers practical help and hope.

All around us, there are barriers and walls that have come up. But let's say you help somebody get on the right path economically, and for whatever reason, they reject the profoundly spiritual things. Still, you have been the hands and feet of Jesus Christ. Jesus healed people. Did all of them end up being disciples? Absolutely not. But He healed those who could not walk, could not speak, or who were possessed. Was it a good thing? Was society helped? Were families strengthened? Absolutely, just by the kind acts and the healings that were done.[2]

The Clock Is Ticking

Because of the gap in support, instead of going back to his lifesaving work, Tom found himself scrambling to find a way to keep his promise of support to Alex and Priscilla. The couple only had sixty days to move, and the clock was ticking. Alex told him that everywhere he went, he was being asked for large sums of money to secure an apartment. He and Priscilla would be happy just to rent a studio or a room, but that wasn't working out either. Tom could sense the stress in his voice.

Tom asked Anna for financial help for the couple, and she responded generously. He went across the street from the abortion clinic, where Christians often gathered to pray, and asked them for help. They were surprised that he had to do this. They had also thought that those kinds of needs were being taken care of by the pregnancy center. When they found out that it's not that simple, they all gladly gave.

Thank God that Tom was able to gather enough money to help Alex and Priscilla secure a deposit for an apartment, but it took weeks to gather the money—weeks that Tom could have spent in front of the clinic saving other lives. Eventually Alex and Priscilla moved into their new apartment, Alex's employer put him back on full-time status, and Priscilla had a beautiful baby girl.

RENEW tried to work with the couple to help them build a stable home for their baby to grow, but they lived too far from us, they didn't have a car, and it was very difficult for us to connect with them in person on a regular basis. Sadly, shortly after the baby was born, their relationship fell apart. Alex still pays child support and occasionally visits the baby. Priscilla managed to buy a used car and drives for Uber to support herself.

While we're glad Priscilla and the baby have some financial support, this is not the outcome we had hoped for. We had hoped to pass the baton to Christian mentors who would model a healthy marriage relationship, lead the couple to a relationship with Jesus Christ, and travel the journey of life alongside them. Unfortunately, there weren't Christian mentors available in Priscilla and Alex's area. We still pray that God will provide the mentorship they need.

Often the baton handoff from the resource center to the Church isn't a smooth one. It can feel like there is no one on the other end to pick up the slack and confront the reality that bringing a child into the world requires navigating the challenges of poverty and the lack of resources.

As more people become aware of these needs, I believe more churches will get involved in pro-life support ministries. In doing so, the church will significantly impact the community, and couples like Priscilla and Alex will fare far better.

4

Creating a New Normal

If motherhood is a labor of love, then single motherhood requires double the labor and double the love.

Unknown

In 1993, I was married and had two beautiful sons, a four-year-old and a two-year-old. My marriage was a difficult one. I felt like it was filled with delusional jealousy and verbal and emotional abuse. I'm not the type of woman to tolerate this kind of treatment for long, so I suggested marriage counseling, but I remember my husband refusing to go. He is from a different culture and country, and it seemed like he didn't see anything wrong with his behavior. I realized things were not going to change, but I couldn't just ask for a divorce, and I feared he would take my boys abroad and I would not be able to get them back. So I made an escape plan.

I opened a bank account, and without him knowing, I slowly started to funnel money into it. I was able to accumulate ten thousand dollars in that account, and my plan was to take the money and my boys and move to a part of the country where the cost of living was more affordable. I would have money to start off with while I was looking for a job, and I was confident I would not have a problem getting a job. I had built up a significant skill set in the years I spent in the information technology field. I had money, I knew where I was going, and I had contacts there who would support me. All systems were a go! Or so it seemed.

Then I realized my period was late. I anxiously took a home pregnancy test, and it came back positive. My world turned black. I felt sick and angry. Self-hatred bubbled up inside of me and gripped my throat as if it were choking me. But mostly, I felt trapped. My mind was racing, and the only solution I could think of was to kill myself. I wanted out of this situation, this marriage, this life, and I wanted out now! How would I do it? When?

Thankfully I looked to my left and saw my boys sleeping. I couldn't do that to them. They would grow up thinking that their mother was a coward and had left them to be raised by a father who would teach them to be just like him. I could stand the thought of that even less than the thought of staying in my marriage. So suicide was not an option for me, but I was still trapped. I needed a plan B, and that was an abortion.

I grew up in the church, and I was attending church at the time. I knew abortion was a sin, I knew it was murder, but I also knew that both of us could not survive. It was either me or it—this unborn child who was the only thing standing between me and my freedom.

For the next few days, there was a battle inside of me. My thought of *You can't do that—it's murder, a sin!* was followed by *But you'll die, your plan will die, your hope for a new life will die!* All I saw was death. It was either me and my hope for a life of peace, or the baby inside of me. One of those things had to go—I couldn't see both surviving. I was in so much anguish that my words can't do justice describing it. If you've felt this anguish, you know very well what I mean.

A few days later, I told my mom I had to run some errands and asked her to watch the boys. When I dropped them off, she asked me if I would go to the bodega on the corner and pick up ingredients she needed to make dinner. On the walk back from the store, I tripped on the raised sidewalk and went sliding face first on the concrete. My hands and knees were a bloody mess. I limped back home and broke down in tears. My mom thought I was crying about the fall, but I was crying because I had been about to make a huge mistake by having an abortion, and I felt God had stopped me.

Eight months later, I still felt trapped, but as I held my daughter in my arms, I felt joy for the gift God had given me. Life truly is precious. Yet I also felt shame that I would've chosen my life over hers. I looked at her beautiful face and thought that I couldn't let her grow up in the chaos I lived in. What kind of role model would I be? I was a shell of my true self as a woman. I had to figure another way out.

Longing for More

Often an abortion-minded woman melts into tears when I ask about her future. I have been guilty of thinking, *Come on, don't be selfish! You can make an adoption plan. In nine months, the baby will be born, and you can go on as normal.* But what if she doesn't want to go on as normal? What if she wants something different? When my daughter was born, I didn't want to go back to normal either, but I had the resources and support to make a change. Women sitting in a pregnancy center often don't.

I've heard my clients say, "I don't want to be a statistic." They know the statistics. They know that they're becoming a part of those dreaded numbers, and they don't want that because it brings shame, guilt, and self-hatred. They're becoming the very thing they never wanted to be. Amanda, the young woman from chapter 1 who emailed me seeking help, later explained:

> I had expectations for my life when I found myself in this pregnancy situation. But I thought everything was going to work out because I was with this good guy. But then my family falls apart—my mom, my boyfriend, everybody. I found myself getting bits and pieces of furniture donated from people or stuff left on the curb. So literally, the stuff I had, I had gathered. I was thinking, *I'm a gatherer now.*

I was trying to do my best, but I was not making it. How could I bring a child into the world when I couldn't even provide for myself?

I felt lost. I was hearing people say that a baby was a lovely gift from God, that pregnancy was a magical experience, but it didn't feel that way for me. I felt like a burden, a beggar. I was dependent on people to survive. I felt like pregnant garbage. That was a rough time in my life.

It was painful for me to hear Amanda's words. They broke me. Unfortunately, her perspective is not uncommon for women feeling trapped in a harsh, heavy, and isolating world.

It Takes a Village, Right?

Pregnancy centers do a great job of providing support from conception throughout the nine months of pregnancy and often through the baby's first year. But those of us who have had children can look back at our first year of parenting and realize that those months were the easy part. Fortunately for me, I remarried an amazing man who took my children as his own. I can't imagine raising my children without my husband's support, as well as that of my mother and my sister Millie.

You might be thinking, *Don't the women you serve have mothers or sisters?* Probably, but in generational poverty, familial support systems aren't consistent or reliable. Everyone is busy doing what they must to survive. In my interview with Dr. Payne, she frequently mentioned how poverty's instability makes it nearly impossible to plan. If we don't offer a new mom consistent and reliable support, we're asking her to take this life journey alone.

This was what Amanda had to say about needing support:

> Now I understand the saying "It takes a village to raise a child." I often wish I had someone to watch the kids so I can study. Or someone to watch the kids so I can have a couple of hours to recharge before I have to begin another busy week. When I chose to carry my pregnancy to term, I didn't know what I was getting into; I didn't know all the worry and struggle I would go through. What made things worse was that I didn't have anyone to guide me.

Amanda's children are now in elementary school, and she doesn't know what challenges may await her during their teen years. When I think back to my children's teenage years, I'm grateful I had a husband to help with parenting, a church family that prayed for them, and a youth group that provided safe, wholesome, fun, and godly role models. I can't imagine what my children's experiences or my mental and emotional stress would have been like without that support system. Yet we're unintentionally asking women like Amanda to go it alone, to navigate the peaks and valleys of parenting on their own. And depending on how they were parented, the results can be heartbreaking.

Why Are Early and Middle Childhood Important?

Parenting is essential during the critical developmental years of early and middle childhood. We want to help moms stay engaged as parents so their children are not raised by TV, the internet, or video games. We want to help parents in poverty gain the skills they need to feel confident in their role as they raise and discipline their children.

As we delve deeper into the world that poverty creates, it is important to define what we are looking at and how it affects parenthood. The Office of Disease Prevention and Health Promotion breaks down the different phases of childhood and demonstrates the pivotal developmental role of early and middle childhood. Early childhood is generally defined as the period from birth until the child's sixth year of life, and middle childhood is typically the ages of six to twelve. In those formative years, children are exposed to an enormous amount of change, new experiences, new ideas, and new environments. They build the foundation of their social and emotional abilities, which impact their physical and emotional well-being along with how well they learn and how much value they place on their own health. Similarly, they begin to forge physical and cognitive skills, making giant leaps in language development, socioemotional skills, cognitive reasoning, and physical manipulation and ability.[1]

While physical growth continues in middle childhood, more profound skill development determines how well a child interacts socially with others. As they change from children to young adults, they begin to take on other roles and relationships that can prepare them for a productive life as an adult.[2] Research reveals that children's experiences from these first two stages of development, for good or bad, will shape a lot of what they are able to do over a lifetime.[3] A child's preparation for school, work, and future life as a successful contributing member of society is directly correlated to their early experiences.

Failure to provide a healthy environment for developing children can cause long-term damage, and childhood trauma, including poverty, can lead to many health problems in adulthood.[4] Childhood is particularly critical to brain development, as the human brain grows to some 90% of its full size by the age of three. In this early stage of life, not only are children learning to problem-solve, communicate, and move about, but the bedrock of their emotions—things like trust, kindness, and love—are formed, along with their opposites. Negative factors such as poor care, unsafe living conditions, and the burden of expectations beyond their ability can severely delay or damage healthy development. And the damage is not temporary. Imagine a skyscraper with cracks in the foundation. Building another fifty stories on top of it isn't going to make it any stronger. Eventually, the skyscraper will have problems that will severely damage the whole structure.

Positive role models and caregivers, along with a safe environment and emotional support, translate into the best chance for a child to live their best life. They will be equipped to form skills that lead to academic success, self-discipline, healthy diet and exercise habits, risk avoidance, and the ability to form healthy relationships.

The foundation for all these vital skills forms during the first decade or so of a child's life. Yet single mothers seldom have the necessary support to ensure their children can cultivate those critical developmental skills. More often than not, a single mother has to pay someone else—a daycare center or a sitter—to ensure her children are fed and taken care of during the long hours she works to make ends meet. A mom in poverty often struggles to keep herself healthy, motivated, and determined, and finding the energy to provide developmental support to her children can feel overwhelming, so she engages these challenges through the path of least resistance.

Permanent Parenthood

As pro-life advocates, we invite young women and men into the permanent reality of parenthood. So when we ask women to make the permanent choice for life and parenthood, we need the Christian community to come alongside them and commit to being a part of the parenting journey, to be part of the process from poverty to stability, and to help usher both mother and child into an abundant and hope-filled life.

The primary parenting support that moms receive at RENEW is through their one-on-one mentoring relationship. Additionally, we've found that our workshops addressing other issues significantly improve a mom's parenting by alleviating depression, anxiety, hopelessness, and financial strain so moms are more emotionally present and engaged with their children.

For example, during a conversation with her mentor, Darlene, a mother of three, mentioned that her daughter didn't want to go to school and was giving her a hard time. Darlene was frustrated. Her mentor suggested, "Why don't you talk to the teacher about it?" Darlene didn't see any point in doing that because, as she said, "Nothing would change anyway." When the mentor saw her resistance, she asked some questions and realized that the thought of meeting with a teacher was very intimidating to Darlene, especially as someone who didn't have a high school diploma.

The mentor explained to Darlene the importance of being an advocate for her children and pointed out that if she didn't intervene now, things could get a lot worse. She said she would be happy to coach Darlene on how to address her concerns with the teacher. That would give her the opportunity to frame her concerns in a direct and respectful way. They could also develop some questions she could ask the teacher about solving the issue.

Darlene hesitantly agreed. After the coaching and practicing, she was ready to make an appointment to speak to the teacher, but she made a request for her mentor to accompany her to the meeting.

When the appointment date came around, Darlene's mentor accompanied her, but she didn't say a word to the teacher. Darlene did all the talking, and she did a great job. The teacher was grateful that Darlene had made her aware of her daughter's issues in class, and they quickly developed a plan to fix them. Darlene left the meeting ecstatic and enthusiastically thanked her mentor as she gave her a big hug.

That experience empowered Darlene. It gave her a sense of confidence and pride that she could advocate for her children and make things better for them. Now, whenever it's necessary, Darlene calls the school, schedules appointments, addresses her concerns, and gets results all on her own. She just needed someone to show her how to do that and to be present for support the first time.

Mentoring can make it possible for parents like Darlene to become actively engaged in parenting and feel energized to continue the difficult task of raising children alone and in poverty. As mentors, we also want to encourage co-parenting and, when possible, marriage. Yet without the proper preparation, counsel, and support for a couple, a marriage will not provide the physical, emotional, and financial safety it was designed to bring to families.

For example, a single mom has a boyfriend who is her baby's father. He's a great guy, but they do not live together. Instead, she collects food stamps and gets medical insurance and a rent subsidy from the government. As Christians, we may be inclined to think that these two should be married and live as a family. I believe marriage could be a wonderful, God-honoring step for this young couple, but without the preparation and support previously mentioned, the results could be less than ideal. Imagine that he is an unskilled laborer making $15 an hour. He might bring home $1,800 per month after taxes. That cannot support a family. Almost all of his income would go to pay the rent. What's left for food and utilities? Perhaps she can get a job as well, but they would have to pay for childcare, and their combined income would push them above the income restriction limit to get significant government aid.

So what's the solution? We are. The Church was meant to bridge the gap. We step up and step in where support—spiritual, financial, physical—is needed. We get involved in families' lives. We role-model what godly marriages and healthy parenting look like. We nurture the young, tender relationships that could blossom into marriage. We use our professional networks and personal connections to help people gain apprenticeships or internships where they build valuable work skills that can lead to economic stability so they can actually care for their families and live dignified lives.

5

The Gospel and Pro-Abundant Life

Transformed people transform people.

Richard Rohr

What does approaching the pro-life movement through the lens of the gospel mean to you? For me, it means to save *and* transform lives. RENEW Life Center was founded in 2013. I thought the Lord was leading me to open a different kind of pregnancy center, one that would invite the Church into greater partnership with the center through discipleship. But wasn't it just like God to show me I wasn't dreaming nearly big enough? I shared what He had put on my heart with several of my volunteers, who had also been raised in poverty. It was something akin to discovering you all shared a secret language or a common experience that forged an irrevo-cable bond. I instantly gained their support in exploring the effects of poverty on women who choose life.

What followed was an incredible journey of remem-bering our past, investigating what causes poverty, and developing a conduit through which the Church can pro-vide ongoing support to women, children, and families in poverty. We wanted RENEW Life Center to be an ongoing support and resource for women who have said yes to life as they face the long journey ahead. Our educational programs, mentoring and discipleship services, and lead-ership training were designed to transform lives, restore hope, and encourage dignity through self-sustainability. We saw that overcoming generational poverty leads to reduced dependence on government assistance, increased self-esteem, and improved relationships.

As cofounders, we agreed that the center should be in an urban area. We searched for a city that didn't currently have a center, and God led us to Paterson, New Jersey. Paterson is the third-largest city in New Jersey and has a poverty rate of 25.2%, compared to a rate of 10.2% across the state.[1] Paterson also has an alarming rate of 65% of births to unwed women,[2] so it sounded like a great place for a pregnancy center.

I decided to call the next closest pregnancy center, which was only four miles away but a world apart from the heart of where I sensed a real need was. I wanted to introduce myself and let them know what our plans were. The ex-ecutive director invited us to meet with her and her board, and we shared our vision of a center that provided services and support for longer than the one year after birth that centers typically provided.

Within days of the meeting, we received a call that Lighthouse Pregnancy Resource Center wanted to partner with us in making our vision a reality. We call our collaboration Paterson Partners for Life. Lighthouse offers medical services, peer counseling, and parenting support, and RENEW provides educational programs and services as well as long-term developmental support through discipleship and mentoring administered by church volunteers.

In hindsight, I'm so grateful that the Lord brought our two organizations together to divide the heavy load of serving women, families, and communities. No one organization can do it alone. It requires the collaboration of the larger Church to serve as God's hands and feet.

That same year, RENEW and Lighthouse staff attended the national Care Net Pregnancy Center Conference together. Roland C. Warren had recently become the new president and CEO of Care Net, and in his keynote address, he shared the new direction he saw pregnancy centers heading. He called the vision he presented *pro–abundant life*, and it was perfectly aligned with the collaboration RENEW and Lighthouse had begun. In an interview, Roland shared his message of pro–abundant life:

> If you're just pro-life, then you can be an atheist and be pro-life, but you can't be an atheist and be pro–abundant life, because if you're an atheist, you're just solving for heartbeats. But if you're pro–abundant life, you're solving for heartbeats that are heaven-bound.

There's an extension beyond that. If a client comes in facing an unplanned pregnancy, and she brings that child into the world, that child has life, but that life is not superior in quantity and quality. You as a Christian are going to say, "Well, that's good, but there's something that's lacking." And that lacking piece is the abundant part of life, as opposed to just life. Jesus wasn't just pro-life. He was pro–abundant life. He said, "I came that they might have life and that they might have it more abundantly." In other words, "I'm pro–abundant life." As a Christian, you can't be just pro-life; you actually have to be pro–abundant life. Because that's what Jesus was.

That leads to why pregnancy centers can't fulfill the full pro–abundant life mission on their own. The pregnancy center can help with evangelism, but the pro–abundant life perspective is not just evangelism. It's also about discipleship.

Through relationships, we can help women and their partners transform how they view marriage and family life and guide them in making godly decisions that bring about a positive impact on their spiritual and earthly future. Thinking about it that way leads you to more of a discipleship model, which is where the Church comes in. The Church has the opportunity to use the pregnancy that a woman is facing as missionary work; it's a mission field.

It's like if the woman at the well went to the pregnancy center. It's the same kind of concept that Christ didn't leave her where she was, her life was transformed, and she got reconnected physically, emotionally, spiritually, and socially.

When she went back to the town after that transformation, she wasn't an outcast anymore. She wasn't coming back to the well during the hottest part of the day, all alone, at risk and vulnerable. Why? Because she got reconnected into the community. We know that because when Christ came to her town, hundreds and hundreds of people were saved, and if they truly were saved, then who helped connect them to Christ? It was her! So you've got to believe that the next time that she went to the well, she wasn't by herself, that she was reconnected into the community of women. She was reconnected to the community and to society. She was transformed.

That's the piece that's really important. It's really the extension where the pregnancy center then entrusts the woman to the church and the people within the church. When the people in the church start to think about this more from a discipleship standpoint, they realize that we need to walk alongside this person. This is what it means to be in a discipleship relationship; you're going to be helping that person with their physical, emotional, spiritual, and social needs. And that is not a temporary relationship; it's an ongoing relationship where you're trying to get that person to move from the pregnancy to the Church to meet those other needs. Pregnancy centers can't do all that. They're not designed to do that. The pregnancy center is primarily focused on mother and baby from conception to birth; they are not designed to fulfill the Great Commission.

We're not just trying to make sure that a child has life. We want to make sure that a child has abundant life, consistent with God's design. This is why we have to connect those we serve, both men and women, to the Church.

When Jesus engaged people, what did He do? The first thing He did was have compassion for them. He met them at their point of need. And that offered them hope.[3]

I love Roland's message. It confirmed to me and to Lighthouse that we were headed in the right direction. At RENEW, we seek to present this pro–abundant life to women through grace-filled, compassionate discipling and mentoring.

Pro-Abundant Discipling

Oftentimes in pregnancy centers, women come to Christ. Through their twice-a-month visits, they develop a relationship with their peer counselor where they hear the gospel and make a decision for Christ. That's fantastic, but we can't stop there. That young woman needs discipleship. If she's not discipled, then she may be saved, but her life may not be transformed. Christ's commission to the Church was to go and make disciples, not to *only* go and lead people to salvation or go save babies. That means that our commission is to make disciples of the mother and her child so they can have an abundant life in Christ *and* help them overcome the trauma of abuse and the vicious cycle of generational poverty. In this way, we apply the fullness of the gospel to our pregnancy center ministry and the Church.

Biblical principles are easy to teach but sometimes difficult to apply to our daily lives. For example, believers may teach a woman that sex outside of marriage is a sin—that God designed sex for marriage. It's a simple concept to understand, but it's not easy to live out when marriage and families are nonexistent in that woman's community. We also know that families in poverty without a male in the household are at greater risk of being victims of violence, so we must remember that the man in her house meets her need for protection. How can she apply the principle of sex only within marriage without support and role models to help her?

As we approach this ministry with the gospel, we also have to approach it with much grace, understanding that this woman is not living a life like ours, in our environment with our safety and resources; she's living a completely different life. She may want to be obedient in that area of her life, but she may not feel safe acting on it at the time.

We need humility and grace to seek to understand what life looks like in this context and in the culture and communities we are serving so that we can approach them with awareness and understanding. This understanding allows us to see that perhaps some choices are made out of necessity due to pressures that we don't have to grapple with on a day-to-day basis. Some of the choices for survival may challenge our moral values, but the reality these women face requires these difficult choices to ensure survival, and humans are always going to choose survival.

When we have a clear understanding of the environment that the women we serve are living in, we can't say or think things like, "Now that you know better, do better." The journey from hurt and bad habits to hopefulness in Christ is a long and sometimes messy one. It requires our steadfast support to keep the women and men we serve stumbling in the right direction.

Dr. Ruby Payne's book *A Framework for Understanding Poverty* explains that poverty is a culture, and culture is part of the very fabric of our lives. To remove ourselves from culture, from a way of being that has been ingrained into who we are, is a very difficult thing. There are going to be lingering elements that affect people even as they move out of poverty. So at RENEW, we seek to focus on what we know is the right path and point people in that direction, and we recognize the need for a huge space of grace. While we don't condone a poor choice, we acknowledge that we are all powerless without the help of Jesus Christ and those investing in our lives. The women we serve need someone they can reach out to when they are wobbly in their walk, someone who will help shore them up when they want to go back to the habit or the behavior that kept them from living their most abundant life. Our support must be a commitment to come along for the long and messy haul.

One of our workshop participants corrected me once when I said that knowledge was power. She said, "No, knowledge is not power; applied knowledge is power." That was a huge eye-opener for me because I realized that just because we taught women something or modeled a behavior didn't mean they were able to apply it to their lives. They could know something but not be in the environment to apply it; there are obstacles and sometimes even dangers associated with applying knowledge in certain environments. We have to demonstrate patience and grace when we see that a woman knows things and has even seen us model them but does not yet have the ability to apply them.

In Scripture, we see how Jesus walked with the chosen twelve, and there were many times he said, "Let me remind you of what I taught you. How many times do I have to teach you this? Remember when I showed you how to do this?" Even with Jesus modeling for them and living with them, He had to constantly remind them. He specifically invited those He'd called to leave their environments, come away, and walk a journey with Him. They were invited to eat and sleep and be on the same path together. Even with that level of intimacy, the disciples were prone to return to their past behavior. They would forget what they had been taught or could not apply what they had just seen. Despite their inability to conform to the teaching they had received, Jesus demonstrated boundless patience and grace, modeling perfect mentoring and discipling relationships.

Pro-Abundant Mentoring

At RENEW Life Center, we use the term *mentoring* because if we ask a young woman who is struggling to survive if she wants to be discipled, the answer will most likely be no—she has other things on her mind. But if we offer her mentoring to help her reach her goals, the response is most frequently yes. Our prayer is that mentorship turns into discipleship, and more often than not, it does.

Much of the mentoring we do feels like parenting parents. Individuals who have chosen parenthood don't necessarily have the upbringing to be a responsible parent. In the same way we parent our children by lovingly teaching, repeating, and reminding, we are, with respect for their age, parenting the parents we serve. This "parenting" is not inviting them into a relationship with a hierarchy; instead, it is coming alongside them as their equal. It's an apprenticeship, a mentorship, discipleship. We respect them for the individuals they are and acknowledge that they are separate and different from one another. We are not personally responsible for them, but we have a responsibility to serve them because we have a responsibility to our Savior Jesus Christ.

A mentor is someone who helps another person learn the ways of the world or specific tasks. In a similar way, Christian discipleship helps a person learn the ways of Christ. At RENEW, a woman may have a primary and a secondary mentor and, at times, a tutor as well. She gains a group of people to surround her and support her in her journey. It's not a mentor's job to solve the woman's problems. Rather, the mentor helps her find solutions and guides her in developing problem-solving skills. Ultimately, a mentor should help her create SMART (specific, measurable, achievable, relevant, and time-bound) goals, as well as provide guidance, support, and encouragement as she sets out to meet milestones that lead to a healthy and stable home for her child, and ultimately to a relationship with Jesus Christ.

You might think of missionaries as people who serve outside our country, but we seek to be missionaries in our urban cities just a couple of miles away from our homes. It's a full-time job for some people, and it's a volunteer opportunity for others. Either way, we are grateful for the staff to provide the long-term care that we want for these young families.

If we open our eyes and hearts to the pain, suffering, and abuse these women and children have endured, if we allow God to use us as part of His plan to redeem and restore, we will see a greater number of lives transformed and connected to the community that is the Church, and we can even see whole cities transformed.

She's Not Alone

I was in my office one day when a local school nurse called and said the mother of a couple of boys in her school was in her office and needed a lot of help. Another mom in the school had told her that the pregnancy resource center she was visiting had referred her to RENEW Life Center and that our classes and mentoring changed her life. Although the people we target are women and men referred to us by the pregnancy resource center, we also get calls from other sources looking for support services for women. The nurse asked about our Getting Ahead program and wanted to know if we were still accepting applications. I told her a class was starting soon, so the woman in her office had to come in that day to fill out an application and get interviewed for consideration.

About an hour later, a petite and very thin woman walked in. Julides looked like a frightened little girl. As I sat across from her during the interview, I could see her hands were trembling, and I sensed God telling me to hug her. That was a strange thought for me. I'm not a hugger, especially when it comes to strangers. And besides, this was a professional interview. I wasn't going to hug her.

Hug her! I felt God say again and again, and repeatedly I thought, *No.* This internal dialogue went on throughout the entire interview.

Julides shared that she was on the verge of being evicted for the seventeenth time in five years. She had no family in this country, and the boys' father had abandoned them a long time ago. It was clear to me that this woman did not need a class. She needed a miracle, an advocate to intervene and try to secure viable housing for her and her children. I told her that she could join our class and that I would accompany her to court for her eviction hearing to see if there was anything that could be done.

As I reached out to shake her hand, the words "hug her" were still swirling around my heart. As she was about to walk out the door, I said to her, "Hey, can I give you a hug?" She darted back and hugged me like she was clinging to a life preserver.

At that moment, I felt the bottomless pit of need she had, and it wasn't just the immediate need for a secure home; it was so much more. She sobbed as she held me. I had to fight back tears. She thanked me for the hug and said she really needed it; she couldn't remember the last time she was hugged.

The court date came around, and I accompanied Julides to court. She thanked me profusely for going with her. I told her I didn't know if there was anything I could do to help, and she said, "That's okay. I'm just glad that I'm not here alone." That's all she wanted—not to be alone.

It was soon her turn before the judge, and he ruled that she had to pay $3,200 before 5:00 p.m. or she would have to vacate the apartment. I asked for more time to try to come up with the money, but no, 5:00 was the deadline.

I run a small nonprofit and didn't have an extra $3,200, so I took her to Catholic Charities, thinking that they could help her immediately. But unfortunately, they said it would take a couple of weeks for them to get a check to her. Next I took her to the Department of Children and Families. I explained her situation and asked if they could help her; the response was no. I asked if they could place her and the boys in a shelter. The caseworker responded that they were out of shelter and motel vouchers, and then she added, "If she can't find a place to stay, we'll have to take possession of the boys."

I was shocked at the callousness of this caseworker. It's easy to assume that social services are in abundance, that shelters are free and safe, and that anyone can just walk into one at any time. This couldn't be further from the truth. While I stood there feeling helpless as Julides wept, she told me again that she was grateful she wasn't alone.

Three days later, I pulled up to her house, and there she stood on the sidewalk with her two boys and all her possessions out on the curb. I asked her what was going to happen to all her things, and she said, "Once I leave, the neighbors will pick through my stuff and take what they want." This was surreal to me. I had never seen or experienced anything like it, but now I know that it goes on every day in cities across our country.

I couldn't bear the thought of Julides losing everything again, so I suggested that she select what was most important to her and put it in my minivan. We couldn't save everything, but we could save some of her more treasured items. Once the items were loaded in the van, I drove her and her boys to a motel for the night, bought them a pizza and some soda, and told her I'd see her the next day to continue trying to figure out what to do.

As I drove home, I felt sick. Was this the best I could do for them? Was this the best the body of Christ could offer the widow and the orphan? It was a long, restless night for me, but I'm sure it was far worse for them.

Julides and her kids spent several days in the motel while we tried to find a solution. RENEW was paying $120 a night for the motel, but we couldn't do that for much longer. We got excited when a donor offered to cover the security deposit and first month's rent for an apartment for Julides and her boys, but we didn't know how she would keep up with the rent. She hadn't finished high school and did not have any marketable job skills. The only job she ever had was cleaning, and she couldn't afford an apartment on just that. And because of her long list of evictions, no one reputable would be willing to rent to her without a huge up-front payment.

The money I had for the motel was drying up quickly, and I lay awake in bed wondering what would happen to this family if we couldn't find a long-term solution fast. Then I had a thought: just down the hall in my house were two empty bedrooms—they had been empty for years. It would be crazy to bring people I didn't really know into my home, right? But if you come from a background of poverty like my husband and I do, it's not so crazy. We both remember times in our childhood when someone we didn't know was sleeping on the couch or even on the floor. There's an unspoken rule among the poor: you always share what you have because you never know when you'll be the one with the need. My husband had heard me talk about Julides and her boys for several days, and he knew how my heart was broken for them. So when I asked him if I could bring them home with me just for a few nights while we figured things out, he didn't hesitate to say yes.

I could still cry when I remember Julides's face as she sat on the bedroom floor at my house. She didn't want to sit on the bed. She was a broken mess of a woman. She felt ashamed to be taken in by strangers, she felt guilty for what she had put her children through, and she felt rejected and abandoned by the man she thought had loved her. I didn't know what to say to her, so I just sat next to her and said nothing. She looked at me and thanked me for not leaving her alone.

Three years have passed since that night, and Julides and her boys are still living with us. I can't begin to tell you how they have blessed our lives. God has taught me, my husband, and our nineteen-year-old son so much through this experience. He used it to mold us and teach us how to love the way He loves. It wasn't always easy.

Early on, there were times when I was so frustrated with Julides. I would think, *Why isn't she getting things done quicker? Why can't she make up her mind? Why is she still crying over that man? We've opened our home to her, and she doesn't have to worry about being on the street. We're providing everything for them, so why doesn't she take advantage of this opportunity and get her GED?* The questions went on and on, and my frustration grew and grew to the point that I wanted to throw my hands up in the air and give up on Julides. But every time that I wanted to tell her this was not working out, I could sense God asking me, *What would happen if I gave up on you?*

I came to terms with the fact that she was not my project to fix. I just had to love her like God does—unconditionally. So I began my journey of learning to love Julides unconditionally, regardless of whether she met my expectations, simply because she was God's daughter and He had entrusted her to me that day He said, *Hug her.*

The best way to help transform someone's life is to love them like God does. If Julides and her boys leave my house with nothing else, I want them to leave knowing Jesus. They go to church with us every Sunday. The boys attended the youth group and quickly made friends. I sent them to a Christian camp during summer vacations, and one of them received Jesus as Savior! Julides has expressed a desire to be baptized, she got hired at a local daycare center, she has passed two out of the five courses for her GED, and she's a beautiful, vibrant woman who I now call my daughter. Her boys say that they're living their dream life, and she says I'm the mother she never had. And I have an even bigger bonus family. God and Julides have taught me so much through this experience—things that I don't think I could have learned any other way. It has been messy, frustrating, and glorious. God is so good.

I'm not advocating that everyone should take women and children into their homes. This is just my story. But ask yourself, *How can I be a part of someone's transfor-*

mation journey? How can God use me to bring love and hope where there is none?

Jesus with Skin On

During a mentoring session, a young woman shared that her baby's father had walked out on her. As she cried, I placed my hand on top of hers. She leaned over, put her head on my shoulder, and said, "Marisol, you're like Jesus with skin on." I asked her what she meant, and she said that Jesus was invisible and I was the closest thing to Him that she could touch or hug.

We must love and live like Jesus. At RENEW, our greatest desire is to point these women and families to Jesus. We want them to see and feel Jesus through our mentoring care for them. Veronica, one of RENEW's longtime mentors, explained the vital role mentors play in the development and transformation of the women we serve.

> When the women we serve cry out for help, that cry is not, "Where are You, God?" Rather, it is, "Who are You today?" They are essentially asking, "What form is help embodying today? Are You a pastor today in my crisis? Are You my mentor today in my situation?"
>
> When a woman is going through a difficult time, asking her to hold on to the feeling or knowledge that God is with her is not enough. She needs more than a feeling; she needs physical evidence. She needs to take hold of someone and feel their presence, an actual body. It has to be someone who she can see with her eyes, who she can truly be in the moment with, talk with, and relate to so that she can say,

"God put this person in my life at that moment to impact me and get me through that season." Then when she looks back, she can say, "When I was going through something, God put a mentor, God put a sister in Christ in my life."

In reality, it's not just a person He put but a true servant of God who could be filled up by Him to be used in her life at that moment. God does this because she needs that more than a feeling. For God to be real, she needs evidence of God, such as a servant of God appearing in the flesh. We can tell her to pray and read her Bible, but sometimes a still, small voice isn't enough; sometimes it has to be a person. The best example of that is Jesus Christ Himself.

God talked for thousands of years, and the time came where He had to come in the form of a human being to embody the Son of Man and be the Son of God so that we can relate to Him. The knowledge and feeling of God weren't enough; religious leaders weren't enough. That's why today we have Jesus Christ. We also have ambassadors of Christ around us all the time. They are called believers.

In 1 Corinthians 14:33, Scripture says that God is a God of order, and He wants to be able to pour into the lives of these women so that their lives can have order and they can continually walk in the way that He has for them. The only way they can replicate this in their own lives is to have a living example. Where is that example constantly being played out? In the church! How are they going to know the God of order and peace if they're not connected with His Church?[4]

Being connected is not a one-way street, however. Getting someone to come to service on Sunday will not create a connection or transform their life. They may find moments of faith and hope in that service, but the only way for real transformation to occur is for them to be in a relationship with those in the Church—brothers and sisters in Christ who are committed to showing their faith through their actions, not just their words.

What is your threshold for offering support and guidance to single moms or co-parenting couples in your church who are just keeping their heads above water? This type of discipleship is the core way to alleviate poverty, which is not done by money or policy but by the body of Christ investing time and energy in those who struggle spiritually and economically.

Representing Jesus well and approaching ministry through the lens of the gospel is far easier in theory than in practice. In over twenty years of ministry, I have found that when humanity is on full display, it can be messy and hard to endure. In those moments, we must embrace Galatians 6:9: "Let us not become weary in doing good, for at the proper time we will reap a harvest if we do not give up" (NIV).

6

Short-Term Support versus Long-Term Sustainability

Our success in influencing others is in proportion to their belief in our belief in them.

Henry Drummond

How did we get here? How did this happen? Those were my thoughts after reading Amanda's email. We did a great job of leading her to choose life, but then we dropped the ball. My particular pregnancy center at the time didn't have many resources to offer her, and maybe other pregnancy centers would have had the ability to give her the items she'd listed without much difficulty, but the real need was greater than that. She needed to be reassured over and over that she had made the right choice, and nobody was doing that for her. There was no soothing voice, no reassuring person walking with her through the wilderness she found herself in.

In a recent conversation with Amanda, I mentioned to her that at the time I received her email, I had been in ministry for eight years, and in those years, we had served at least seven thousand women.

Me: Why did it take seven thousand women for me to get one email like yours?

Amanda: I almost didn't send that email. I sent it because I thought that hearing "No, we can't help you" would be easier for me. Or if I did not receive a response from you, it would be an obvious NO. I would then know that I'm not going to waste my time and ever go back there again. Plus, my pregnancy was high-risk at the time, and I was bedridden. I needed help, I couldn't get up, and emailing you was my only way to reach people who I thought could help me. I knew about Planned Parenthood, but I wasn't sure if they had anything to offer me besides an abortion. At that moment, I was not sure about continuing with the pregnancy, and I know they were good at persuading you to abort. I was still at the stage where it was possible to do it; I was afraid they would talk me into it.

Me: What would have happened if I hadn't responded?

Amanda: I was looking into possibly placing the baby for adoption. But the only thing is, I don't know if I could've lived with myself.

Me: Why do some women believe that having an abortion is easier than making an adoption plan?

Amanda: Because you will always know that your child is out there, and you will ache to be with your child. You will have a hole in your heart for the rest of your life. Because of that, we think it's easier to abort and shut our conscience. It's the same reason why some women don't want to sell their eggs, although they can get five to ten thousand dollars for them—a piece of them would be out there. They could make money off it, but they still don't do it.

Me: I'm glad I responded.

Amanda: Yes, me too. I slept with the laptop open, hoping you would respond.[1]

Pro-Life Ministry Reimagined

When my team and I were praying over the development of RENEW, God impressed these verses from the book of Isaiah upon my heart:

> The Spirit of the Sovereign LORD is on me,
>   because the LORD has anointed me
>   to proclaim good news to the poor.
> He has sent me to bind up the brokenhearted,
>   to proclaim freedom for the captives
>   and release from darkness for the prisoners,
> to proclaim the year of the LORD's favor
>   and the day of vengeance of our God,

to comfort all who mourn,
   and provide for those who grieve in Zion—
to bestow on them a crown of beauty
   instead of ashes,
the oil of joy
   instead of mourning,
and a garment of praise
   instead of a spirit of despair.
They will be called oaks of righteousness,
   a planting of the LORD
   for the display of his splendor. (61:1–3 NIV)

In these verses, we saw God's answer to our prayer. Here is how we personalized the verses:

The Spirit of the Sovereign Lord is leading and
   equipping us, because the Lord has called us to
   share the gospel with single moms and couples
   who have chosen life.
He has sent us to help put back together the
   broken hearts of women who feel betrayed and
   abandoned, by pointing them to Jesus.
We are to proclaim freedom from condemnation
   and the oppression of poverty, to bring light and
   hope for those suffering from loneliness and
   depression.
To teach them to trust in God's grace and mercy
   and to rest in the assurance of His promises.
To comfort all who mourn the loss of
   relationships or the future they fear is lost
   because of the unplanned pregnancy.

> We are to place on them a crown of beauty instead
> of shame, the oil of joy instead of mourning,
> and a garment of praise instead of a spirit of
> despair.
> They will be restored and called strong and
> magnificent, known for their integrity, justice,
> and right standing with God—a work of the
> Lord, that He may be glorified.

The first three verses of Isaiah 61 became our marching orders. We founded RENEW Life Center to be a vehicle through which the Church can reach women like Amanda and fill the gap that exists between the choice for life and the lifetime ahead. In collaboration with the Church, we hope to assure these single women and couples that they have a continuous stream of support and constant access to physical, emotional, social, and, most important, spiritual resources. Because their families and immediate communities cannot meet their needs, the body of Christ must support these people.

Our Agendas versus God's Will

In her email, Amanda stated that her family became too busy for her. We can all relate to being busy. I'm sure as you're reading this, you are also thinking of a few other things you should be doing instead. I know that my natural tendency is to want to get things done; checking items off my to-do list gives me great satisfaction. And when I'm in the groove of getting things done, I hate to be interrupted.

I once shared my frustration over being interrupted with Joan, my pregnancy center director, and she responded with, "Did you know that most of Jesus's ministry was an interruption? Jesus was usually on His way somewhere or teaching and even praying when He was interrupted with a request to meet a need." Wow, I had never noticed that before. From then on, when I read my Bible, I looked for the interruptions that were occurring in Jesus's life on earth. I learned that He valued caring for the lost and hurting more than getting to His destination on time or any other item on His agenda.

If we loosen our grip on our to-do list just a bit and allow God to interrupt our busy lives, we can significantly impact women like Amanda and even entire families. First John 2:17 reminds us, "This world is fading away, along with everything that people crave. But anyone who does what pleases God will live forever" (NLT).

At RENEW Life Center, we have created an environment where single moms and families can feel supported by believers who provide guidance for the journey that lies ahead. Families come to RENEW looking for help in becoming self-sustaining. Being dependent on the government is dehumanizing, and nobody wants to be on welfare for a lifetime. Some individuals are believers, and others are not. As we help them achieve the self-sustainability they want most, God often opens the doors for us to share the gospel message with those who don't know the Lord and to disciple those who do. When we view discipleship as something that grows their relationship with the Lord *and* helps them take steps toward creating stable homes and achieving self-sustainability, we demonstrate that we care for every aspect of their lives.

Poverty and Shame

I remember when I was a little girl, my mom would have me miss school so I could accompany her to her welfare appointments. Back in those days, a Spanish-speaking social worker was a rarity, and we did not have translators. I remember the dirty plastic chairs, the grueling questions, the condescending looks, and the obvious shame my mother felt. I had to translate things for her that she probably never wanted me to know. I remember the long, silent walks home. I shared her shame.

Today, in some ways, these types of situations are even worse. There are plenty of bilingual social workers, but instead of having to share her most intimate details with just one social worker, a woman in need must share them with three. There is one social worker for her cash assistance (TANF), one for her food stamps (SNAP), and yet another for her housing assistance (TRA). Every time she sees a different social worker, she relives her trauma and shame. At some point in her life, she may think that self-sustainability is not an option; it's just not attainable for her. The longer she stays in poverty, the harder it will be for her to get out. If she is in situational poverty for one year, she has a 56% chance of overcoming it, but after seven years, there is only a 13% chance that she will ever be able to achieve economic stability.[2] If a woman like Amanda, who now has a master's degree and a full-time job, is still struggling to be self-sustaining, can you imagine the chances of a twenty- or thirty-year-old woman trapped in generational poverty without a high school diploma?

From Surviving to Thriving

According to the Guttmacher Institute, one of the top three reasons for having an abortion is the inability to afford a child.[3] We often hear stories of young women born and raised in poverty who are aspiring for more. When they're faced with an unexpected pregnancy in college, their world falls apart, and their dreams for an outcome better than what they were born into are in great danger. We want to inspire these women to believe that achieving economic stability is possible while choosing life.

When poverty is generational, it's a chronic condition that keeps churning out more poverty until something positive happens that interrupts the cycle. RENEW is that "something" that is interrupting poverty for our families. So how do we do that? We have curated workshops and Bible studies that address the special needs of the women and families in poverty.

Money & Me: This financial literacy workshop is created specifically for low-income adults.

Mom as Gatekeeper: This workshop helps break down barriers between mothers and fathers by addressing what is known as maternal gatekeeping. Maternal gatekeeping is common in impoverished homes where children have been raised solely by their mothers. Young women have been raised to believe that a father isn't really necessary, but in our workshop, we help them revise their parenting practice.

- We increase the mother's awareness of what gatekeeping is, how it operates, and how it is sometimes misused out of anger and hurt.
- We offer concrete examples that will help mothers understand the negative impact of excessive gatekeeping and the importance of supporting father involvement.
- We engage mothers in exercises that help reduce restrictive maternal gatekeeping behaviors that inhibit father involvement.

Think Differently: Beyond our behavior, our thinking more than anything else determines outcomes. If it's plagued with misconceptions about God, faith, family, sex, finances, etc., it leads to the many problems the women we serve face. This Bible study brings these issues to light and teaches that our only hope for renewing our minds is in God alone.

Leadership Development: Various leadership development workshops help our moms and dads reach their peak potential in every area of their lives—professional, vocational, parental, and spiritual.

Getting Ahead in a Just-Gettin'-By World: This is our main workshop, and we believe it is foundational to getting people out of poverty. What makes Getting Ahead different from other workshops is that the focus is not on poverty symptoms such as unemployment, homelessness, and limited education. Instead, it addresses the root causes of poverty, which can be summed up as a knowledge gap. A knowledge gap is information or skills not taught in schools because most educators assume children learn these things at home:

- expectations of the academic environment
- time management
- real-life problem-solving
- how to balance a checkbook
- how to budget
- how to apply for a job
- work ethics

The list can go on and on—everyday things that most kids learn at home simply by observing their parents. Our workshop addresses these topics and provides practical steps and tools to overcome this gap.

Programs that address the symptoms of poverty are critically important, but the problem is that they're building on an unstable foundation. We end up with people who have an education, a job, and a home but are still operating from a survival mindset. It's only a matter of time before everything falls apart and they're back at square one. For example, Amanda had a college education, an advanced degree, and a career, and in her words, "I was doing what I was supposed to be doing." Yet she faced many of the same challenges as those who don't have an education or career. Why? Because poverty does not end with a college education or a job. It ends with a mindset shift. The Getting Ahead workshop helps the participant make that shift.

The Getting Ahead workshop is intense, and it's not for everyone. To participate, individuals need a referral from their Lighthouse peer counselor or another RENEW partner agency. Then they have to complete an application, which is followed by an interview. We follow this process because the truth is that helping people overcome poverty is expensive, so we don't merely want to fill a seat; we want to bring about real results. We are looking for women and men who are ready to face the hard truth about their economic condition, to dig deep and analyze how they contributed to their current situation, and to explore how community conditions and government policy have also contributed to chronic poverty. And finally, we are looking for people who are ready, willing, and able to make *big* changes in their lives.

Once they're accepted into the program, the journey begins! For the next ten weeks, we read, research, and report on the causes of poverty. Understanding what causes poverty helps participants from generational poverty understand how their family of origin functioned and how they got to where they are today. Although raised in poverty, I never really understood it until I went through the training to teach the Getting Ahead material.[4] As I did, my upbringing and my parents' choices began to make sense. I quickly realized that there is a huge knowledge gap in poverty that most people don't know exists, not even the poor themselves. The workshops discuss basic life skills that would be common knowledge for most middle-income teenagers, but concepts like planning for your future are eye-opening for our participants.

One comment we frequently hear in class is, "Why don't they teach us this in school?" The answer is that schools assume it's taught at home. As a teenager growing up in poverty, I didn't know that my future was up to me. I didn't know that I could dream, make choices, and make plans that would lead to a successful life because how to plan for the future was not taught in my home. I'm sure that somewhere during my childhood I must have had teachers tell me that I could do and be anything if I set my mind to it, but I didn't believe them because my home life didn't reflect that message. That message was for other people, not girls like me.

In the Getting Ahead workshop, participants learn that to get out of poverty, they must own eleven key areas of their lives. The workshop goes far beyond finding employment; we also address the support and resources needed for them to keep their job, advance their skills, and create relationships that will foster their social and mental growth. They also learn that different environments operate from different sets of rules of engagement. In the academic and professional world, the rules of engagement are based on achievement. How does someone from generational poverty successfully navigate that environment when the only rules of engagement they know are based on survival? Our workshops properly equip families to enter unfamiliar territory and navigate it with confidence. And after completing our Getting Ahead workshop, graduates can choose to be paired with tutors or mentors who will serve as friends, guides, and role models on their journey to faith and self-sustainability.

Getting By before Getting Ahead

Getting out of poverty is hard work, and it's scary, especially when the safety net of government assistance is quickly disappearing. Once a mom enters the workforce and is fortunate enough to get a childcare subsidy, her other benefits such as SNAP and TANF begin to decline. Although social workers will tell you that it is a slow decline, those on the receiving end would not agree.

Take Gina, for example. When she first came to Lighthouse for a pregnancy test, she was already a mom to three small children. She had been born and raised in Paterson, and although she had her first baby as a teenager, she managed to graduate from high school and get certified as a dental assistant. Life was going pretty well for her, so she decided to pursue her lifelong dream of moving to North Carolina to give her children a better life. She moved with her three children and her boyfriend, and for a while, life in North Carolina was great. They had a lovely apartment with a playground for the kids, they both had jobs, and they were even able to buy a used car.

Then the car broke down and they didn't have the money to fix it, so Gina started taking the bus to work. Unfortunately, she had to walk the kids to school and then grab the bus to work. The bus schedule did not align with the time she had to be at work, so she was often late. Her boss gave her a warning about her lateness, so she explained her situation and requested that her schedule be adjusted, but he did not budge. After several warnings from her boss, she was fired. With no car and no job, she could not make rent payments and eventually got evicted, even though her boyfriend was working and contributing to their expenses.

Then her boyfriend disappeared. Why? Maybe he wanted to be with Gina only when it was easy and didn't want to deal with the chaos. Perhaps overcome with a sense of helplessness and frustration over their situation, he felt so impotent and ashamed that he couldn't face her and the kids. We don't know. But all Gina could do was stuff her children's backpacks with all the clothes she could squeeze into them and get on a train back to Paterson. She had no choice but to move into her parents' house, which was a very toxic environment. Her family mocked her for daring to dream of a better life. "We knew you would be back with your tail between your legs," they arrogantly told her.

Shortly after her return to Paterson, Gina suspected that she was pregnant, and she ended up at Lighthouse sitting across from me. By this time, I had served in pregnancy center ministries for fifteen years, so when I tell you that this was one of the hardest intakes I have ever done, I don't say that lightly. It was as if Gina was drowning, and I was a life raft that she could cling to just long enough to share her story before she lost her grip. But instead of going under, she was pulled up onto the raft and heard, "It's going to be okay; we've got you."

Gina's pregnancy test was positive, which left her feeling fear and despair. How could she have another baby now? I told her about Lighthouse's programs that would provide emotional and material support throughout her pregnancy and the baby's first year. Then I told her about RENEW's programs and services that would support her as she got back on her feet and help her come back even stronger and more stable than she was before. She asked me how long RENEW would provide emotional support and guidance. I told her for as long as it takes for her and her children to feel safe and secure. And even after that, I would hope to have the privilege of watching her family flourish. Through her tears, I saw a little comfort and a spark of hope.

Gina wanted to sign up for our Getting Ahead class right away. I told her she should wait until after the baby was born because her due date was during the course's tail end, and she would miss out on the final sessions. It was our fall session, and classes were on Mondays and Thursdays. She insisted and made her case: "I'm due right around Thanksgiving; if I give birth between the Monday before Thanksgiving and that Friday, I can be in class on Monday. I would only miss two sessions, and I can make up the missed assignments."

Was she kidding me? Although I thought it was impossible, I loved her excitement and enthusiasm. I didn't have the heart to say no, so against my better judgment, I enrolled her in the class.

Gina started the class, had incredible breakthroughs, made new friends, received tons of love and encouragement, and gave birth the Wednesday before Thanksgiving! And just as she promised, she showed up to class on Monday morning.

By the time Gina graduated from the workshop, she was on fire! She had three job interviews the week after graduating and acquired a full-time job the week after that. Great story, right?

But wait, there's more . . .

A full-time job brought new obstacles that, without RENEW's support, Gina wouldn't have been able to overcome. The first obstacle was childcare. Childcare costs are as much as $225 per child per week, with several months' waiting period in some states. If a mother is fortunate enough to apply without being placed on a waiting list, she still must provide two weeks' worth of pay stubs to get approved. So how does she pay for childcare during those two weeks? Thankfully because of the donations we received for our Bridge the Gap Fund, RENEW covered the cost of Gina's childcare for that time. If we had not, Gina could not have accepted the job.

The second obstacle was the reduction of her SNAP benefits. Gina was doing such a great job at work that she got a raise from $15 to $17 an hour. That's cause for a celebration, so we celebrated!

A month later, Gina showed up at my office looking frantic and told me she had to quit her job. "What?" I said, surprised and confused. She told me that she'd received a letter from her SNAP benefits saying now that she'd had a pay increase, they would reduce her benefits from $700 a month to $450. She was panic-stricken; her safety net of public assistance was rapidly disappearing. "I can barely make it as it is. How am I going to do it with less?" she cried.

This was the logic behind her wanting to leave her job: She would retain her $700-per-month food benefit and would also get temporary rental assistance. She might also get some cash from TANF, but even if she didn't, she had guaranteed food and housing for her children.

Gina wasn't crazy; she was actually "poverty smart." Our current regulations and policies for these assistance programs discourage people from working. It's safer and even saner to depend on the government for survival than to go out there and try to make it on your own.

As Gina explained her situation, she kept saying, "I have to quit! I have to quit!" I tried to calm her down, but nothing I said mattered. Not knowing what else to say, I finally blurted out, "No! You're not going to quit, and I promise you, you and your kids will have plenty to eat." As soon as the words left my mouth, I thought, *What did I just say? How am I going to keep that promise?* But it worked. Gina calmed down and went back to work; she trusted me. Now I had to figure out how I was going to keep my promise.

RENEW was founded to be a vehicle through which the Church can serve moms like Gina, so I reached out to the women's ministry team leader from a church that regularly supported our ministry and told her Gina's story and the promise I'd made. She immediately sprang into action, shared the need with the women's group, and developed a plan to provide weekly groceries to replace what Gina had lost by continuing to work. At the same time, Gina connected with a RENEW mentor who took her and her children to church.

This is the gospel in action. This is what a comprehensive approach to pro-life ministry looks like. And as Roland Warren would say, this is what it means to be pro–abundant life.

The Bridge out of Poverty

Even with all this support, Gina is still struggling to provide food for her children, pay rent, and maintain a self-sufficient lifestyle as a single mother, but like all the women we serve, she's stumbling in the right direction.

The diagram below shows how quickly the safety net of necessary benefits, such as food stamps, rent subsidies, and

Crossing out of Poverty

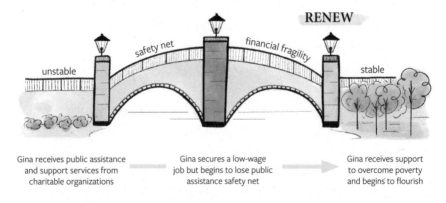

Gina receives public assistance and support services from charitable organizations

Gina secures a low-wage job but begins to lose public assistance safety net

Gina receives support to overcome poverty and begins to flourish

childcare, is lost long before financial stability is achieved. Getting out of poverty is hard, breaking bad habits is even harder, and replacing an old mindset with a new way of thinking and living takes steadfast effort—and time. It takes much more time than the RENEW team would like, but we commit to serve women like Gina with the same patience and grace God shows us all. No matter how long the journey takes, every new skill and every new mindset change are passed to a mother's children. The concepts, skills, and tools that she's learning in her twenties or thirties, her children learn at a much earlier age.

Kerri, one of our first Getting Ahead graduates, said, "Since graduating, I have accomplished so much! One of the things I am most proud of is that after being unemployed for eight years, I finally have a job I love! I went from not having any confidence and feeling like my life was out of control to now walking with my head held high. Even more exciting is that I can pass on all I have learned to my children so they will have a leg up starting off their lives."

That's not just one life transformed; that's lives changed for generations to come. For the women and families we serve at RENEW, knowing that they have people in their lives who care about their spiritual growth, their dreams, and their goals and will connect them to the resources needed to accomplish those goals means the world to them. It gives them hope for the future they have always dreamed of attaining.

One thing is sure: poverty is very lonely. Many of our graduates have found their best friend among the participants in the Getting Ahead workshop. They finally have a friend who wants the same things they do: a better life for themselves and their children. They've found a friend who will not criticize them for wanting more out of life, a friend who will cheer them on. Combined with their relationship with their mentor, the RENEW staff, and a church, these friendships create a community around the graduates that provides role models, resources, love, acceptance, and safety.

Invisible Resources

Most people who are considered middle-income have resources that are almost invisible to them, so they can sometimes take them for granted. But for someone in poverty, access to those resources can be the difference between surviving and thriving. For example, you may have a network of friends, colleagues, and other professionals you can tap into when you have a need. Let's say you're looking for a job, so you contact a couple of old colleagues to see if they are hiring at their company. Or perhaps your friend owns a landscaping company, and you ask him if he can give your teenager a summer job. Those natural opportunities are resources that people in poverty often don't have.

Now imagine if you shared your network with someone in poverty—you ask your friend who owns the landscaping company if he would give your mentee an internship at his office to practice the office skills she's learned and have some experience she can put on a résumé. When you donate clothes to the Salvation Army thrift store, you might see it as gaining extra space in your closet, but for the mother who can buy those clothes at a low price and keep her kids warm all winter, it's nothing short of a miracle. When you donate a lawn mower to a church member trying to start his own lawn care company, you are nurturing his right to dream and his desire to begin paying for his own needs.

When those of us with more connections and resources practice habitual generosity, a woman starting in poverty can move from where she is to where she aspires to be.

Transformation Requires the Church

The women who visit Lighthouse Pregnancy Resource Center have the good fortune of stepping not just into a beautiful, state-of-the-art facility but into one that recognizes their long-term needs. There's a seamless transition between Lighthouse's pregnancy services and RENEW's long-term support through workshops, leadership development, mentoring, and discipleship. Our collaboration has led us to see spiritual and financial transformation in the lives of the women we serve. But in order for those transformations to happen, we are heavily dependent on the Church. We require a small army of volunteers who genuinely want to build a relationship with these women— not take them on as a project or mission but genuinely befriend them for a season and maybe even a lifetime.

Yes, I said a lifetime. Nowadays, that seems a little extreme. We live in a culture where we think microwaves are slow. We live with the idea that if we do our "job" well, we can get it done quickly and move on to the next person or the next mission. We have been conditioned by "day of service" events to develop a tourist mindset of our Christian life of service, seeing it less as a pilgrimage and more as a DIY project. We want casual commitments and immediate results. We desire the outcomes derived from discipline but fail to invest our time, preferring instead to fast-forward to the fruit without nurturing the root. I'll admit that I was unknowingly falling into that mindset even while I was working in ministry. I wanted quick results.

As the RENEW family, donors, prayer partners, and volunteers walk alongside moms and families, they will learn more about themselves and God than they ever could have imagined. It is our long apprenticeship to grow in holiness. For me, it's in service to these families that I am able to see the biblical principles that I hear my pastor preach about on Sunday come to life on Monday, Tuesday, Wednesday, and every other day of the week. It's in serving that I am able to pour out what has been poured into me. Serving in ministry as a volunteer and on staff has been the fertile ground God has used to grow and develop my faith.

So how can the Church get involved in this daunting but rewarding mission? The first step is to learn about poverty. If you're thinking, *I grew up in poverty, so I know all about it*, I promise you, you don't. I truly did not understand my family dynamics and the effect poverty had on all of us until I read Dr. Payne's book *A Framework for Understanding Poverty*. There are many other helpful and insightful books on the topic, some of which are listed in "Resources for Helping People in Poverty" at the end of this book.

Even as I encourage you to keep learning about poverty's impact on our communities, I want to caution you about two things. First, don't get stuck on learning and feel you have to read every book ever written on the subject before you can act. And second, don't just learn from books; you can also learn by jumping right in and creating relationships of mutual respect with people in poverty. They have so much to teach us.

To fill the gap between the choice women and men make for life and the lifetime after, we need the body of Christ to use their unique gifts to help us provide the educational workshops and services these families require to grow in Christ and in economic stability. There is a role for everyone.

Is your heart leaning toward serving women facing an unplanned pregnancy and parenting concerns? Then contact your local pregnancy center. There are many volunteer roles for you to choose from.

Do you have a special interest in helping teen moms? YoungLives is a ministry of YoungLife focused on reaching teen moms by entering their world, modeling the unconditional love of Christ, and encouraging them to become the women and mothers God created them to be.[5] If your local pregnancy center doesn't already have a YoungLives club, how about you and your church start one?

Maybe it's the thought of the hardships caused by poverty that grips your heart, and you want to help moms create economically stable homes for their babies to thrive. Contact RENEW and get plugged in to one of our many volunteer roles. If your local pregnancy center doesn't offer expanded services like those provided by RENEW, then why not look into starting something similar?[6]

Partnering to Bring Hope

Christian life isn't a one-person race. It's a relay. You are not alone; you're part of a team assembled by our unstoppable God to achieve his eternal purposes.

Christine Caine

One of the most common verses used in the pro-life movement is Deuteronomy 30:19. You may be familiar with it: "This day I call the heavens and the earth as witnesses against you that I have set before you life and death, blessings and curses. Now choose life, so that you and your children may live" (NIV). It wasn't until recently that I realized there wasn't a period at the end of verse 19 and that verse 20 starts with "and." It continues with "that you may love the LORD your God, listen to his voice, and hold fast to him."

There is more to choosing life than living! The "and" is what this book is all about. It is also the "why" behind the work of RENEW and the reason we are so passionate and unapologetic about challenging Christians to see the bigger picture and participate more fully in the mission of pro–abundant life. I agree with Roland Warren, president of Care Net, when he says we should be "solving for heartbeats that are heaven-bound." Making life choices possible is crucial, but if our services and support stop there, families will likely face a messy, hard life that is not well lived. I get excited when I read Deuteronomy 30:19 and let myself slide right into verse 20; that's where abundant life begins. It begins with loving God, listening to His voice, and holding fast to Him.

The Pregnancy Center's Role

I interviewed Debbie Provencher, executive director of Lighthouse Pregnancy Resource Center in New Jersey. She explained the role that pregnancy resource centers should play in the comprehensive approach to pro-life ministry:

> The pregnancy center comes alongside someone making a pregnancy decision. Our role is to help this person or couple assess their physical, emotional, and spiritual needs and strengths as they're making this important choice. We want to equip them with the resources to be able to choose life and to thrive as parents.
>
> We're looking at their entire situation, and we're helping them slow down to do this too. As I think about this,

when people debate the abortion issue, when they talk about abortion and its rightness or wrongness, they're often approaching it from a theoretical standpoint. We're actually helping the real women and men who are making these decisions in the midst of complex situations. They're making these decisions with pressures from the outside, the experiences in their life that have shaped them, their family of origin, their current circumstances, and especially the people in their lives right now who are either supportive or not in favor of this pregnancy. That's everything that comes to bear on their decision.

We're trying to help them look past the immediate fear, past the immediate circumstances and pressures to get a bigger, better perspective. Sometimes the woman or couple needs help to realize that they already have the resources within them, but fear is clouding their judgment. It just takes someone to slow them down and say, "Wow, the fact that you came here today looking for help means that you're already thinking like a mom. You started taking prenatal vitamins already because you care about your child's well-being."

We are really helping parents get to the heart of who they are, to be able to sort through the complicated emotions that they're feeling. We don't want to see them make a quick decision they will regret, or a decision they can't commit to once they walk out our doors.

I think most pregnancy centers do a good job caring for the whole person. We recognize, like Jesus did when He stopped His preaching to feed the 5,000, that people can't hear us if they are hungry. They're not going to hear anything we're saying about life or about the gospel until we take care of their most immediate needs. Jesus cared for people's whole needs, not just their spiritual needs. He took care of their physical needs too.[1]

While pregnancy centers meet many of those immediate physical needs, their role or mission is not to dive deep into them, so women and couples face a gap in care. Debbie recognizes this gap and addressed the misconception that after a woman walks into a pregnancy resource center, everything's going to be okay:

> There are needs our parents have that are greater than any one nonprofit can meet, or are outside the scope of our mission. At a staff meeting last week, at least four of the prayer requests were for women who are feeling pressured by their housing situations or financial hardships. One pregnant woman was happy just to be sleeping on a friend's couch, but that friend is getting evicted from her apartment.
>
> Most of the challenges our moms face are related to housing and economic needs. Many of them are in unhealthy or abusive relationships, but they're tied to that person because of a housing need, or they're tied to their parents because of housing needs. The biggest need I see over and over again is the need for affordable, adequate housing for a mom and her child.
>
> I remember ten years ago, I spoke with the director of a nonprofit ministry that offers housing and education assistance to first-time moms. It was a wake-up call for me because I was neglecting that piece of the overall picture. Many pregnancy decisions are connected to the woman's housing situation or to the person providing housing for

the woman. So it's all related to economics. If a person can't get a job that adequately pays the rent, then what?

If a mom wasn't already working, she would have to look for a job, and if she's very pregnant and if she already has another child to care for, you're thinking, *This just isn't going to add up.* It's mainly financial needs that are a pressing concern. We offer material aid related to the pregnancy and to caring for a newborn. On occasion, we provide some emergency financial assistance for rent or utilities. But that assistance is a bit like giving someone a fish today without equipping them to fish for tomorrow and the day after that; you're just making them more dependent on you or someone else. This is why we chose to collaborate with RENEW Life Center.

When the founders of RENEW saw the problem of these unmet needs, they thought there must be a solution out there. So they searched and found the Framework for Understanding Poverty curriculum. They identified the problem, but they didn't say, "I have to be the only solution"; instead, RENEW helped find the solution and brought it to the parents we serve. It's what I admired, and why I caught the vision.

As a pregnancy center, we want to excel. We want to improve those things that are within our wheelhouse, so to speak. But if there's a program or a ministry out there that's doing it better, and we can collaborate, then we will be better partnering together. This way, we don't have to create and oversee a whole new program ourselves; we can partner with others who are already doing it.

Since the founders of RENEW had already been in pregnancy center work, they identified a solution to a problem that we had all seen: the overwhelming financial situation so many of the parents we serve face. That's the reason they're coming to the center; it's because they lack the resources for their current or future children. Collaborating just makes so much sense. We don't have to be an expert in everything.[2]

The Benefits of Collaboration and Christian Values

God has equipped us all with unique gifts and talents. We just have to put them to use. When RENEW first began our collaboration with Lighthouse, we quickly realized that our program did not work well for teen moms, but it worked great for young women in their twenties or older. Most teens think they have all the answers, especially teens in poverty who are usually self-parented. They believe they can do the same things their parents did and get a better result. They do not see the connections between their behavior today and future consequences, so they're less likely to see the benefit of RENEW's services. But we still want to help teen moms, so we were excited when Lighthouse added a YoungLives club to their collaborative efforts so that these moms could be reached. YoungLives clubs give parenting teenagers the opportunity to meet mentors. Clubs offer fun, laughter, encouragement, Bible studies, and outings. As the saying goes, teamwork makes the dream work.

But make no mistake: even with an enthusiastic team it isn't easy, especially if these women, whether teens or young adults, grew up in generational poverty. And we know it's hard sometimes to get someone to focus on more abstract spiritual things while she's drowning in concrete problems. So, at RENEW, we listen to our participants, we find out what issues are most pressing for them and what their hopes and dreams are, and then we help them address those issues. We develop a relationship with them through our workshops and mentoring that are designed to help them overcome poverty. Some participants will overcome poverty and others won't, but we pray that all will develop a lifelong relationship with God. Having a relationship with Jesus Christ will not only transform them spiritually but also transform their experience in poverty.

Poverty can be less traumatic and damaging if a person grows up in a household that upholds Christian values. Because of my mother's faith and our church involvement, there was never any money spent on alcohol, cigarettes, lottery tickets, and countless other vices that negatively impact families. We were taught biblical moral standards, which were strictly upheld, and so avoided the damage caused by teen sex and pregnancies. My mom protected us from making the same mistakes she had. Sure, Christmas gifts were minimal. We mostly shopped at thrift stores and never had a vacation, but the rent was always paid, and there was always food on the table. And my mom tithed from her welfare check and sent $20 monthly to World Vision for her sponsored child. In contrast, my friends who grew up in secular homes experienced teen pregnancies, drug addictions, evictions, and a host of other issues.

A Christian's experience of poverty in the US, although still filled with difficulty and shame, tends to be less traumatic. People of faith living in deprived neighborhoods experience better overall well-being than their nonreligious neighbors living in the same area.[3] That's why I believe that how successful we are at getting families out of poverty comes second to how successful we are at getting them to know and grow in Jesus Christ.

Debbie Provencher explains why programs like RENEW Life Center and YoungLives are so important in light of spiritual realities:

Pregnancy centers have gotten very professional and highly organized with policies and procedures, and that's awesome. And that's necessary to a large degree, but the more we become like a counseling service, where there's a distance between the people served and those serving them, the less life transformation may happen. Transformation happens when lives bump up against each other. And the most transformation I've seen occurs in people's lives when we've crossed barriers. Our staff has gotten close to many of our YoungLives moms, and as a result, some of them attend our churches. I had the privilege of dedicating one mom's baby to the Lord in our church! All of a sudden, ten people from her family were up on the church platform. It was new territory for them, but we were hugging each other and celebrating life together.

The more the pregnancy center becomes like a counseling agency, the less you can invite your client over for Christmas dinner. But real change happens when people get to see life done differently.

Michelle was a client who visited our Hackensack center. She was a nanny, and if she continued with her pregnancy, it meant she risked losing her nanny position. She knew that if she chose life, she would be facing homelessness. Thankfully a teacher from a local Christian school took her into her home. Sometimes I'd pick up Michelle and the baby's father for church; other times she attended the teacher's church. I feel her life was forever changed because people's lives got enmeshed with hers. She became a follower of Christ and a friend, someone we love and care about. She got to experience something that was a game-changer for both her and her son.

That's why I love these programs that get God's people mixed up in the lives of our moms and dads. No matter how well we serve our parents, we essentially get an hour a week with them. The rest of the time they are influenced by everybody else with different messages, financial pressures, and the stresses of life. We only get an hour a week with them; we need to set them up for success in more lasting and tangible ways. It's like the person who becomes a Christian, and they're trying to live the Christian life, but they only spend an hour in church, with nothing outside of that all week to nurture them.

[Typically,] one of the difficulties in getting a woman to visit a church is that she's stepping into a completely different environment, and she feels alone and out of place. But when you have these RENEW mentors and relationships, where you start becoming friends and then an invitation to church is extended, the level of trust is already there, and a mom or dad is more likely to say yes. I personally haven't seen a good result with just saying, "Here's a list of churches; pick one."

We want to transition these women and their partners from the pregnancy center to the church, but you need to have a bridge between them. Programs like YoungLives and RENEW Life Center are that bridge.

Our clients' lives don't change overnight; we don't change our own lives overnight! If I want to be a better person, if I want to lose weight or start exercising every day, it takes a lot of work to turn the ship around. So why do we expect the people we serve at our center to quickly snap into a new life? It really takes getting people into their lives. We need caring Christian people interacting with these women and men day in and day out, encouraging them, so they don't go three weeks without hope. They could bring them along to church and invite them to women's or men's groups—things that open the door to new possibilities for them.

To that end, Lighthouse launched a new program called Birth of a Family. It's a weekly program to invite the women and couples we're serving to come and learn what marriage and healthy relationships look like. We want to give them a picture of what the benefits of marriage are and give them more support in their life. RENEW is excited to support Lighthouse in this new endeavor, but we need the partnership of local Christians as well.

James 2:14–17 says, "What good is it, my brothers and sisters, if someone claims to have faith but has no deeds? Can such faith save them? Suppose a brother or a sister is without clothes and daily food. If one of you says to them, 'Go in peace; keep warm and well fed,' but does nothing about their physical needs, what good is it? In the same way, faith by itself, if it is not accompanied by action, is dead" (NIV).

A pregnancy center is about deeds and about action. The material support and the parenting support that we provide are very practical, but again, they're temporary. An organization like RENEW that really reinforces a long-term positive change in people's lives *and* that will still be in relationship with them three, four, ten, or twenty years down the road is another tangible way of meeting physical needs. The physical needs we meet at the pregnancy center are related to the nine months of pregnancy and caring for a newborn, but who will help meet the needs of the family when the child is five and ten and eighteen? The more we surround that family with relationships that outlast the pregnancy and the baby's first year of life, the better the outcomes we will see.[4]

Pregnancy centers meet a woman in her time of crisis. They offer a compassionate ear, medically accurate information, an ultrasound to confirm pregnancy, and a glimpse of her baby's beating heart—plus a host of other services. The center looks for opportunities to share the gospel, and they collaborate with other partners who can help lead a mom to a local church. They pass the baton to the body of Christ.

Believers provide not only the spiritual support but also the community support that so many families desperately crave. We now get the opportunity to play a part in a mom's and baby's journey to an abundant life where they can realize their dreams. Does that excite you? I hope so.

One Phone Call Changed Her Life

In chapter 6, we met Kerri, who, after eight years of unemployment, finally has a job and is now feeling confident and proud of herself. But that's not the whole story. Kerri was living a self-identified double life. Her children's father was very abusive, and she had been living under those terrible conditions for more than fifteen years. We all suspected it, but she never confirmed it. She had recently shared, "It's like I'm two people. During the day at work, I'm in my element, and I'm feeling whole, but as I approach my house, my demeanor changes." She hadn't realized that change until Mary, a coworker, gave her a ride home one day and mentioned that she saw her countenance change as they approached her house.

Kerri didn't make much of Mary's comment, but what her coworker saw was enough for her to be concerned. A couple of days later, Mary decided to call Kerri at home to see how she was doing. What she heard in the background confirmed her suspicions: Kerri was living in a domestic violence situation. When she saw Kerri at work, she pulled her aside and said, "I'm not going to force you into anything, but what I heard going on in your house is abuse. It's not good, and it's time for you to get out."

Kerri later shared that what Mary said impacted her because it gave her situation a name. Up until then, it was just life as normal for Kerri.

Get out? she wondered. But how? And where? Could she afford an apartment on her own? Kerri had another coworker, Linda, who helped her with her budgeting. She finally worked up the courage to ask Linda if she thought she could afford an apartment independently. Linda answered no and asked why Kerri had wanted to know. Kerri finally broke down and told Linda everything that was happening at her house. She told her about the violence and explained that her teenage daughter had to take medication for depression and anxiety, her son was just a shell of a boy, and her toddler walked around covering her ears. Linda, a Christian, told Kerri that she had suspected something was going on, and she had been praying for her.

Up to this point, Kerri was afraid to ask for help because she thought no one would believe her story. I could see why. I had met her partner, John. He was tall and very good-looking, had a great smile, and was a charmer. But I could see right through him. She told me that he frequently made comments like, "You're lucky I'm letting you work"; "You better _____, because if I leave, everything will fall apart"; and "You should know how I am and be used to it." But my personal favorite was, "If you hadn't changed, I wouldn't be acting this way."

That's right, John, she had changed. That change began on a September morning when she sat in our classroom for her first day of the Getting Ahead workshop. I still remember her sad eyes. She seemed nervous and very timid, but over the next ten weeks, I saw her transform into a confident, hopeful woman. When she got a job, she took off like a rocket, and John didn't like that.

So when Kerri shared with Linda what was going on, Linda asked her, "Do you want to leave?" And Kerri did. So Linda called her pastor and explained the situation. He said he would have an emergency board meeting that night and get back to Linda with a response. The next day, he called back, and Kerri had a home to go to with her children.

The pastor's swift response was possible because his church was part of the Family Promise Network (FPN). FPN is a network of churches that provides temporary shelter and support to working families with children who are experiencing homelessness or domestic violence. The shelter provided comes in different forms. Sometimes it's space within the church, and other times it's a house or unused parsonage. This particular congregation had a house they used for missionaries on furlough as part of the FPN. God is so good.

Kerri and her children are now working through the complicated process of rebuilding their lives and healing from their trauma. She's comforted by the assurance that RENEW will be with her every step of the way. I'm grateful that Kerri and her children were rescued from their violent environment, but my heart breaks for the other women we serve who are still waiting for a way out.

Good for Her, Bad for Him

Darlene, whose successes we celebrated in chapter 4, is also trapped in an abusive relationship, and she lives under the tyranny of her children's father. When she graduated from our Getting Ahead workshop, her dream was to get her GED. We helped her set some goals, got her signed up for classes, and assigned her a mentor/tutor who would help her along. But then the fighting started because she was leaving the house too much. It got so bad that she wanted to drop her GED courses. We suggested that if leaving the house was the problem, maybe she could sign up for online classes. The immediate problem seemed solved. But now that she's taking classes online, her partner hides her GED coursebook.

This obstacle might sound like petty stuff, but it exposes the hard truth of Darlene's situation. Her partner wants to maintain complete control over her, and he sees anything she does to improve herself as a personal threat. There's so much yelling, screaming, fighting, name-calling, and threatening that the children are all exhibiting stress and anxiety-related health issues. While Darlene tries to look at the bright side and says, "At least he doesn't hit me," we both know that's not good enough. But as she admits, "It's so ingrained in you that you don't see a way out."

You might be thinking, *Won't a shelter solve this problem?* There are two main reasons why it won't. First, as the Family and Youth Services Bureau reported,

> In just one day in 2015, over 31,500 adults and children fleeing domestic violence found refuge in a domestic violence emergency shelter or transitional housing program. That same day, domestic violence programs were unable to meet over 12,197 requests for services because of a lack of funding, staffing, or other resources. Sixty-three percent (7,728) of unmet requests were for housing. Emergency shelter and transitional housing continue to be the most urgent unmet needs for domestic violence survivors.[5]

Second, unfortunately, shelters are not always safe places. Women who have spent time in a shelter have either been involved in or have seen physical fights break out over things like shampoo or accusations of "your kid hit my kid." Shelters do their best to prevent these types of things, but they still happen frequently. I ask myself, *Is this the best we can do for these moms?* The problem is seemingly insurmountable, but I know that if churches would band together around this issue, we could find a solution.

I regularly check in on Darlene through text messages because her partner gets angry when he sees her talking on the phone. On a Tuesday, I sent her a message to encourage her to continue with her GED online studies, even without her book. Her response was, "THIS WEEKEND WAS UNBEARABLE."

How was I supposed to respond to that? With "I'll pray for you"? I must have said that to her a thousand times in the last five years. I couldn't get myself to say it once again. I shot back an impulsive text: "Darlene, one day soon, you will be out of there, I promise."

There I went again, making a promise I had no idea how I was going to keep. In twenty years of serving in ministry, it was only the second time I had done that. The last time, God provided through His Church. I believe He'll do it again.

The Rest of My Story

After our third child was born, my marriage continued its downward spiral. After one very heated argument, I insisted once again that we see a marriage counselor. I told my husband that I refused to live like this any longer. My response seemed to enrage him, and I remember that just like that, he said he was moving out. Overnight, my life turned upside down. I felt like he was mad that I refused to put up with his verbal abuse, so he was going to make me pay.

Things went from bad to unbearably worse. I had no time for hatching a plan. A few months later, he moved out, but what I didn't know was that he'd stopped paying the mortgage those last few months, and it seemed like he wanted to cause me maximum harm with no regard for how his kids would be affected. So there I was, a stay-at-home mom with three children under five, no plan, and no money. The girl who had overcome generational poverty was suddenly thrown back into poverty, and the crash hit hard. I sold my jewelry to keep the lights on and buy food; I sold my house before it was foreclosed.

Before I decided to be a stay-at-home mom, I'd had a ten-year career in the information technology field, and I had a friend in a job placement agency specializing in IT careers. I spruced up my résumé and sent it to him. The job market was pretty bad, so it took about five months for me to land an entry-level position paying $40,000 a year, which was not bad considering it was 1997. I was relieved, but I didn't know the many other hardships I was about to face. My children's father did not give me any financial support, and because we were still legally married, I couldn't petition the court for child support. I didn't have money for a lawyer to file for a divorce, so I was trapped in financial and emotional limbo.

I wanted to keep my expenses to a minimum, so I decided a two-bedroom apartment would be okay. I would share a room with my daughter, and the boys would share the other room. I quickly found out that no one would rent me a two-bedroom apartment. I needed three bedrooms, they insisted. Some landlords even made me feel embarrassed for suggesting such a thing—a lesson learned. Apparently, it's unacceptable in middle-class neighborhoods for a single mother trying to provide a safe home and great schools for her children to share a bedroom with her two-year-old daughter. Almost twenty-five years later, I still don't understand why that's such an anomaly, and it saddens me to know that the single moms we serve today are facing the same problem.

Given that most landlords require that rent not go over 30–35% of a tenant's income, I knew that I would not qualify for a three-bedroom apartment. One landlord said to me, "I know I'm going to end up having to evict you in a few months." Those words stung, and I felt humiliated.

This went on for months. I couldn't see a way out of this catch-22 until a friend suggested, "What if I cosign for the apartment with you?" Thankfully she insisted, and I finally had to accept her help. Otherwise, my children and I would not have had a safe place to live.

We settled into our three-bedroom apartment in the lovely town of Westfield, New Jersey. The boys started school; I had to pay for a full-day preschool for my daughter. I don't remember how much that was exactly, but I know it was a strain on my budget. I also had to hire someone to pick up my kids after school and take care of them until I got home from work at 6:00 p.m.; that was an additional $150 a week.

I had a tight budget and had to account for every penny. I remember checking out at the supermarket once with my four-year-old daughter. She spotted a hair detangler spray bottle that had Pocahontas on it. She wanted that bottle and begged for it, but it was $4.95! Just a week ago, I had put back a twenty-five-cent pack of gum because I couldn't afford it. Now she wanted this for $4.95. Looking at her face, I didn't want to say no. I wanted her to be happy. I bought the detangler and decided I would figure out how to make up for it in my budget. (By the way, she thought the detangler lasted for months because I secretly kept refilling the bottle with water.)

Twenty-two years later, I still have that bottle. It's a reminder of that challenging time in my life.

Those years were painful. It's by the grace of God that I made it through. It took almost two years to receive regular child support, and I remember my ex-husband fighting me tooth and nail, but eventually he relented, and the money made a huge difference. It was the difference between making my kids a real dinner and pretending to be the cool parent who gave them breakfast for dinner.

The most troubling thing about my story and the reason I share it is that as bad as that experience was, I had it good. I had a skill set to fall back on, colleagues in the industry to help me get a job, a friend who took a risk by cosigning a lease, and eventually the child support due to my children. The women we serve at RENEW have none of that going for them.

I remember one day early in our separation, everything felt out of control. I kept a stiff upper lip throughout the day for the sake of my children, but after I put them to bed, I threw myself on my bedroom floor and cried out to the Lord. "God, I'm no longer asking You for help; help is not enough anymore. I need a miracle." And that was exactly what He gave me—miracles in the form of people He sent to provide the support I needed to get through that difficult time.

The moms we serve are praying for miracles too. Could you be their miracle?

It's Your Turn to Choose

I have talked about the choices women and men must make when faced with a crisis pregnancy and some of the difficult choices they have to make afterward. Now it's your turn to make some choices. You read this book, so you have already made one good choice. I encourage you to make at least one more. Here are a few suggestions:

- Connect with your local pregnancy center and other pro-life support ministries like RENEW Life Center. Take a tour and learn more about what they do to save and transform lives every day. Find out how you can volunteer or donate to support their life-affirming work.
- Be that person who is the answer to prayer for a mom. Just two hours a week of your time can change the course of a mom's life when you make a regular mentorship/discipleship commitment.

- Let's not forget about the men. Husbands and single men are needed as godly role models and mentors to the fathers we serve.
- Become a church liaison. Share our ministry opportunities with your church for funding support and program partnerships.
- Share your gifts and talents with us. There are many non-client-contact volunteer roles to be filled, and this behind-the-scenes work makes a huge impact on the success of the ministry.

I could go on with this list. The needs are many, and I believe the Church is the answer to meeting those needs. If you have made it to the end of this book, you are probably a church member! My prayer is that you're not overwhelmed by the great and ongoing needs in the lives and stories shared here but that you are inspired to become a part of the great work God is doing in pro-life ministry.

In 1 Corinthians 9:24, the apostle Paul compares the Christian life to a race, and he challenges us to run in such a way as to win the prize. I compare pro-life ministry to a relay race where everyone wins—mom, dad, baby—and for certain, you will too. Remember, you don't have to be an expert, and you don't have to do it all. You only have to be ready and willing to open your heart and extend your hand to grab the baton.

Resources for Helping People in Poverty

Corbett, Steven, and Brian Fikkert. *When Helping Hurts: How to Alleviate Poverty without Hurting the Poor . . . and Yourself.* Chicago: Moody, 2014.

DeVol, Philip E. *Getting Ahead in a Just-Gettin'-By World: Building Your Resources for a Better Life.* 4th ed. Highlands, TX: Aha Process Inc., 2020.

Ehlig, Bill, and Ruby K. Payne. *What Every Church Member Should Know about Poverty.* Highlands, TX: Aha Process Inc., 1999.

Keller, Timothy. *Generous Justice: How God's Grace Makes Us Just.* New York: Penguin Books, 2021.

Payne, Ruby K., Philip E. Devol, Terie Dreussi-Smith, and Eugene K. Krebs. *Bridges out of Poverty: Strategies for Professionals and Communities.* 5th ed. Highlands, TX: Aha Process Inc., 2021.

Acknowledgments

Writing a book is something I never dreamed I would do, and although I ultimately found it to be very rewarding, it would not have been possible without my dear friend Sanyika Calloway, who I call my Purah.

Purah was Gideon's servant, but not just any servant. In Judges 7:9–10, God commands Gideon to attack the camp of the Midianites and then tells him to take his servant Purah with him if he's afraid.

I have to admit I know how Gideon felt. I'm often afraid of the tasks God calls me to. I think He knew that because He sent me a fearless Purah in Sanyika. She pushes me, cheers me on, and does not let me back down from a challenge. I will be forever grateful for the long days and nights of her coaching, encouragement, and never-ending support. From the founding of RENEW Life Center to the writing of this book, I couldn't imagine facing these challenges without my sister in Christ, my colleague, and my friend.

I'm eternally grateful to Joan Vitale, who introduced me to pro-life ministry. I still remember the day she handed me a volunteer brochure for her pregnancy center. I smiled, put the brochure in my pocket, and thought, *Fat chance I'll ever get involved with something like that.* Well, long story short, a few months later, I found myself sitting at her pregnancy center's volunteer training, and the rest is history. Joan modeled for me what it meant to be a follower and servant of Jesus Christ. I watched her week after week and marveled at her love for Jesus and her passion for and dedication to the cause of life. I was forever changed by the years I spent serving under her leadership.

When I told my pastor, Tim Chicola, about the burden the Lord had put on my heart, he said, "You should start a ministry to do that."

I replied, "Pastor, I'm fifty years old; who starts anything at fifty?" I should've known better than to have a debate with a pastor.

He quickly shot back, "Moses got his calling at eighty."

Thus began my journey in bringing RENEW Life Center to life. Thank you, Pastor Tim, for your counsel, encouragement, and support, not only in ministry but also in my personal life. I have been blessed by your spiritual leadership and the love and support of my family at The Crossing Church. I thank you all for your generous support in making RENEW a reality. My heart is full.

When I called Lighthouse Pregnancy Resource Center to share the vision for a pregnancy center with expanded services in Paterson, Executive Director Debbie Provencher answered the phone. On the other end of her line was a total stranger with nothing more than a dream. I honestly expected her to hang up on me, but instead, she heard me out because the need was clear to her as well. She invited me to share the vision with her board, and soon after, a pregnancy center "plus" was opened in Paterson. I am so grateful that the Lord brought our two ministries together to bring greater impact to His kingdom. We are truly better together.

God used Amanda to inspire a new ministry and this book. Her unplanned pregnancy, her choice for life, and her desire for a better future for herself and her baby opened my eyes to the needs of women who have taken a leap of faith to choose life. Her honesty and humility interrupted ministry as usual and led me to a broader view of what it means to be pro-life. Ten years later, I am blessed to still be a part of her life's journey, and I pray that I will be for a lifetime.

I am grateful to the women we serve at RENEW Life Center. I have learned more from them than I could ever list here. They generously shared their life stories in this book in hopes that doing so would ultimately help others. I admire their strength and courage to face obstacles and keep striving forward for the brighter future they want to create for their children.

During this journey, I've learned that there's the family you birth, then there's the family God puts together. God expanded my family when He brought Julides and her children, Angel and Jordy, into my life. I am blessed by what I've learned in our journey together and by the love we share.

My adult children, David, Marcos, Sarah, and Jon-Luke, have all used their God-given talents to serve in ministry with me. I thank them for their support in creating beautiful and delicious events for RENEW; facilitating workshops for the women we serve; lugging around heavy, coin-filled baby bottles during baby bottle fundraisers; and generously sharing their mom with others.

Finally, I want to thank my husband, Fernando, my number one supporter and cheerleader. He always has a word of wisdom for me that brings questions, issues, or problems into perfect focus. I can't imagine my life's journey without him.

Notes

Chapter 1 What If Our Pro-Life Perspective Is Too Narrow?

1. Amanda, email to author, November 2, 2010.

2. "Single Mother Statistics," Single Mother Guide, March 12, 2022, https://singlemotherguide.com/single-mother-statistics.

3. Joyce A. Martin, Brady E. Hamilton, Michelle J. K. Osterman, and Anne K. Driscoll, "Births: Final Data for 2019," *National Vital Statistics Report* 70, no. 2 (2021), https://www.cdc.gov/nchs/data/nvsr/nvsr70/nvsr70-02-508.pdf.

4. "Single Mother Statistics."

5. Sanyika Calloway, personal interview with author, July 11, 2020.

6. "Single Mother Statistics."

Chapter 2 Saying Yes in Poverty

1. Ruby K. Payne, *A Framework for Understanding Poverty: A Cognitive Approach*, 6th ed. (Highlands, TX: Aha Process Inc., 2018).

2. Dr. Ruby Payne, personal interview with author, July 16, 2020.

3. Kevin Simon, Michaela Beder, and Marc W. Manseau, "Addressing Poverty and Mental Illness," *Psychiatric Times* 35, no. 6 (2018), https://www.psychiatrictimes.com/view/addressing-poverty-and-mental-illness.

4. Caroline Ratcliffe and Emma Kalish, "Escaping Poverty: Predictors of Persistently Poor Children's Economic Success," US Partnership on Mobility from Poverty, May 2017, https://www.urban.org/sites/default/files/publication/90321/escaping-poverty.pdf.

5. "Teen Pregnancy Prevention," National Conference of State Legislatures, October 11, 2018, https://www.ncsl.org/research/health/teen-pregnancy-prevention.aspx#:~:text=In%20addition%2C%2063%20percent%20of,and%20earnings%20in%20later%20years.

6. "Teen Pregnancy Prevention."

7. Calloway, personal interview.

8. "Fatherless Epidemic," National Center for Fathering, 2015, https://fathers.com/wp39/wp-content/uploads/2015/07/fatherlessInfo graphic.pdf.

Chapter 3 Am I My Sister's Keeper?

1. Lawrence B. Finer et al., "Reasons U.S. Women Have Abortions: Quantitative and Qualitative Perspectives," *Perspectives on Sexual and Reproductive Health* 37, no. 3 (2005): 110–18, https://www.guttmacher.org/journals/psrh/2005/reasons-us-women-have-abortions-quantitative-and-qualitative-perspectives.

2. Tim Chicola, personal interview with author, September 1, 2020.

Chapter 4 Creating a New Normal

1. Kamila B. Mistry et al., "A New Framework for Childhood Health Promotion: The Role of Policies and Programs in Building Capacity and Foundations of Early Childhood Health," *American Journal of Public Health* 102, no. 9 (2012), https://www.ncbi.nlm.nih.gov/pmc/articles/PMC3482035.

2. Mistry et al., "A New Framework."

3. "InBrief: The Impact of Early Adversity on Children's Development," Center on the Developing Child (2007), accessed December 20, 2022, https://developingchild.harvard.edu/resources/inbrief-the-impact-of-early-adversity-on-childrens-development.

4. D. Baumeister et al., "Childhood Trauma and Adulthood Inflammation," *Molecular Psychiatry* 21 (2016), https://www.nature.com/articles/mp201567.

Chapter 5 The Gospel and Pro-Abundant Life

1. "Paterson, NJ," Census Reporter, accessed February 7, 2023, http://censusreporter.org/profiles/16000US3457000-paterson-nj.

2. "Paterson Kids Count: A City Profile of Child Well-Being," Advocates for Children of New Jersey, December 2015, http://acnj.org/downloads/2015_12_10_paterson_kids_count.pdf.

3. Roland Warren, personal interview with author, July 13, 2020.

4. Veronica Cuenca, personal interview with author, September 4, 2020.

Chapter 6 Short-Term Support versus Long-Term Sustainability

1. Amanda, personal interview with author, September 27, 2020.

2. Ann Huff Stevens, "Transitions into and out of Poverty in the United States," *Policy Brief: Center for Poverty Research* 1, no. 1 (2013), https://poverty.ucdavis.edu/sites/main/files/file-attachments/policy_brief_stevens_poverty_transitions_1.pdf?1445548951.

3. Finer et al., "Reasons U.S. Women Have Abortions."

4. Getting Ahead training materials: http://ahaprocess.com.

5. For more information on this ministry, visit https://younglives.younglife.org.

6. These are some of the resources we use at RENEW:

Jobs for Life: https://jobsforlife.org

Money & Me: https://moneyandme.cash

Consumer Resources: https://www.consumerfinance.gov/consumer-tools

Maxwell Leadership Courses: https://www.johnmaxwellacademy.com/store

FatherTopics Booster Session: https://store.fatherhood.org/fathertopics-booster-session-mom-as-gateway

Chapter 7 Partnering to Bring Hope

1. Debbie Provencher, personal interview with author, August 28, 2020.

2. Provencher, personal interview.

3. Pamela Joshi, Erin Hardy, and Stephanie Hawkins, "Role of Religiosity in the Lives of the Low-Income Population: A Comprehensive Review of the Evidence," Department of Health & Human Services, July 2009, https://aspe.hhs.gov/reports/role-religiosity-lives-low-income-population-comprehensive-review-evidence-0.

4. Provencher, personal interview.

5. "Domestic Violence and Homelessness: Statistics (2016)," Family and Youth Services Bureau, 2016, https://www.acf.hhs.gov/fysb/fact-sheet/domestic-violence-and-homelessness-statistics-2016.

MARISOL MALDONADO RODRIGUEZ has served in pregnancy resource center ministries for twenty years, first as a volunteer, then as the director of an urban center. Her years of experience in serving women facing unplanned pregnancies led her to see the many needs and obstacles women in poverty were facing. Burdened by the struggles that confronted these new moms, Marisol cofounded RENEW Life Center in 2013 to fill the gap that exists after the services offered at a pregnancy center end.

Before becoming the cofounder and executive director of RENEW, Marisol worked for the New Jersey Family Policy Council. Prior to that, she worked in the information technology field with corporations such as Verizon Wireless and Prudential.

Marisol is the recipient of the following awards:

The Andy Anderson Award for Outstanding Volunteer Service

The Markee "D" Ministries Supporter of the Year Award

Certificate of Special Congressional Recognition (for outstanding and invaluable service to the community)

Certificate of Recognition from the Office of the Passaic County Clerk (for outstanding contribution toward the Paterson Partners for Life Center in helping families thrive)

The Power of One Life Award (in honor of her generous stewardship of time, talents, and treasure to save and change lives)

Arise NJ Outstanding Citizen Award (for helping families overcome poverty)

Puerto Rican Alliance of Elizabeth Humanitarian of the Year Award

For more information, please contact Marisol:

RENEW Life Center
75 Ellison St.
Paterson, NJ 07505
(862) 257-3817
marisol@renewlifecenternj.org